JOB SAVVY

HOW TO BE A SUCCESS AT WORK

Instructor's Guide

LaVerne Ludden, Ed.D.
Marsha Ludden

Publisher: J. Michael Farr
Project Director: Spring Dawn Reader
Editor: Sara Hall
Cover Design: Dean Johnson Design Group
Interior Design: Spring Dawn Reader

JOB SAVVY—HOW TO BE A SUCCESS AT WORK
©1993, JIST Works, Inc., Indianapolis, IN

99 98 97 96 95 94 93   9 8 7 6 5 4 3 2 1

All rights reserved. No part of this book may be reproduced in any form or by any means, or stored in a data base or retrieval system, without prior permission of the publisher except in case of brief quotations embodied in critical articles or reviews. Printed in the United States.

Ordering Information: An order form has been provided at the end of this book containing other related materials.

JIST Works, Inc.
720 North Park Avenue • Indianapolis, IN 46202-3431
Phone: **(317) 264-3720** • FAX: **(317) 264-3709**

ISBN: 0-942784-80-4

About this Book

This is a book about keeping a job and getting ahead. Based on research into what employers actually look for in the people who succeed or fail, *Job Savvy* is designed to develop critical job survival skills, increase productivity, and improve job satisfaction and success. Using a workbook approach, many in-the-book activities are provided to reinforce key points and develop new job survival skills and plans. The narrative is easy to read and informative using good graphic design, many examples, checklists, case studies, and section summaries.

Why People Need to Improve Their Basic Job Skills

The years ahead are projected to be a time of labor market opportunity and challenge for most workers. Some of these trends include:

- Many new and existing jobs will require higher levels of technical skills.
- The amount of education and training required for jobs will increase.
- Employers will expect their employees to be more productive and obtain better results in more complex jobs.
- More job and career changes are anticipated for the average worker.

All of these changes will require a person who is better prepared than most workers have been in the past. The biggest need, according to most employers and labor market experts, is for workers to have good "basic" skills. These include having basic academic skills, the ability to communicate, to adapt to new situations, and to solve problems. While these and other related skills are not technical skills in the traditional sense, they have everything to do with long-term success on the job. And this is what this book is about.

©1993, JIST Works, Inc. • Indianapolis, Indiana

A Different Point of View

You will find numerous references in *Job Savvy* to the studies and research of psychologists, sociologists and other labor market professionals. Yet this is NOT an academic book. Instead, this information has been used to form the basis for a practical and useful handbook for a working person — or one who soon plans to enter the world of work. Many employers have asked for such a book to give them a tool to encourage their new workers to succeed on the job. And because the author has been both an employer and a trainer of new employees, he brings a unique and helpful point of view that will bridge the gap between an employer's and an employee's expectations. The result of this is increased job savvy where, we believe, both will win.

Additional Photocopies

Several pages in this book are designed as one-page worksheets. If you are using *Job Savvy* as a student text for classroom purposes, you are hereby authorized to make additional photocopies from this instructor's guide as needed to compliment any of the activities.

A Parable

An explorer was once asked what he most disliked about the wilderness. "Is it the wolves?" "No," he replied, "it's the mosquitoes." In a similar way, many people fail on the job as a result of the little problems, not the big ones. This book will help you identify and avoid both, so you can be the best employee you can be.

Table of Contents

Introduction ... 1
Problem-Solving Approach ... 2
  Dealing with Problem Students ... 2
    General Lack of Interest ... 2
    Fear of Formal Schooling ... 2
    The Dominating Personality ... 2
Instructor Preparation ... 3

Planning the First Session ... 5
Getting Prepared ... 5
  Planning a Class Schedule ... 6
  Know the Class Objectives ... 6
  Creating a Comfortable Environment ... 7
  Preparing Materials and Resources ... 7
  Developing a Flexible Mind-Set ... 7
Beginning the First Session ... 8
  Introducing Yourself ... 8
  Introducing the Course ... 8
  Introducing the Group ... 8

Chapter One—Understanding the Employment Relationship ... 11
What Does My Employer Want Anyway? ... 12
  Dependability vs. Reliability ... 12
Employer Expectations ... 13
  Applying What You've Learned ... 14
What Should You Expect? ... 15
Reasons for Working ... 15
Understanding Your Rights ... 15
Resolving Employee Rights Issues ... 16
  Applying What You've Learned ... 17
Summary ... 17

Chapter Two—Your First Day on the Job ... 19
Reporting to Work ... 20
Dress Appropriately ... 20
Starting the Day ... 21
Applying What You've Learned ... 21
Payroll Information and Enrollment ... 21
  Applying What You've Learned ... 21
  Fringe Benefits ... 22
  Applying What You've Learned ... 22
Introduction to the Job ... 22
  Work Instructions ... 22
  Supplies and Equipment ... 22
  Telephone System ... 23
  Breaks ... 23
Off to a Good Start ... 23
  Applying What You've Learned ... 24
Summary ... 24

©1993, JIST Works, Inc. • Indianapolis, Indiana

Chapter Three—Making a Good Impression 25

Wearing the Right Clothes	26	Positive Grooming	29
Dress Codes	26	Good Grooming Habits	29
Appropriate Dress	27	Special Hygiene Concerns	30
Neat Dress	27	Special Personal Considerations	30
Uniforms	28	Mannerisms	30
Safety Clothing	28	Applying What You've Learned	31
Special Safety Equipment	28	Summary	31
Applying What You've Learned	29		

Chapter Four—Punctuality and Attendance 33

Problems Caused by Absenteeism and Tardiness	34	Planning to Get to Work	37
		Applying What You've Learned	38
What's Your Excuse?	35	Getting to Work on Time	39
How Lifestyle Affects Your Work	35	Applying What You've Learned	39
Your Lifestyle and Stress	37	Summary	39

Chapter Five—Learning to Do Your Job 41

Thinking About Learning	42	Continuing the Learning Process	46
Learning How to Do Your Job	43	Education for Life	47
Where to Find Information About Your Job	43	Steps to Learning	47
		Personal Learning Project	50
Example of a Job Description	44	Applying What You've Learned	50
Applying What You've Learned	46	Summary	50

Chapter Six—Knowing Yourself 51

Your Self-Concept	52	Identifying Your Skills	54
Applying What You've Learned	53	Self-Management Skills	55
Learn to Believe in Yourself	53	Transferable Skills	55
How You Look at Life	53	Job-Related Skills	55
You Can Teach Yourself to View Life Positively	53	A Review of Your Skills	55
		Applying What You've Learned	55
Your Job and Your Self-Concept	54	Summary	56

©1993, JIST Works, Inc. • Indianapolis, Indiana

Chapter Seven—Getting Along with Your Supervisor 57

- Work Team Concept 58
- Supervision Is a Job 58
- Your Supervisor Is the Team Leader in the Business World 60
- What Does a Supervisor Do? 61
  - It's Not as Easy as It Looks 61
- Communicating with Your Supervisor 61
  - Rely on Your Senses When Following Instructions 61
  - Asking Questions 62
  - Learning to Ask Questions Worksheet 64
  - Reporting the Results 67
  - Taking Messages 67
- Communicating About Job Performance 68
  - Scoring the Criticism Evaluation Self-Test 70
  - Applying What You've Learned .. 70
- Meeting a Supervisor's Expectations 70
  - Applying What You've Learned .. 71
- Resolving Problems with Your Supervisor 71
  - Conflict Resolution 71
  - Conflict Resolution Worksheet ... 72
- Grievance Procedures 73
- Disciplinary Action 73
- Summary 73

Chapter Eight—Getting Along with Other Workers 75

- Team Concept 76
- Get to Know Your Co-workers ... 77
- How You Fit In 77
  - Applying What You've Learned .. 78
- The Value of Difference 79
- Values 79
  - Effective Work Teams Blend Values . 80
- Temperaments 80
- How to Deal with Differences 81
- Individual Diversity 81
  - Check Your Attitudes 83
  - Scoring Your Attitude Check 84
- Basic Human Relations 84
  - Basic Human Relations Worksheet . 85
  - Applying What You've Learned .. 85
- Special Problems with Co-workers 86
  - Sexual Harassment 86
  - Racial Harassment 86
  - Dating 87
- Summary 87

Chapter Nine—Problem-Solving Skills 89

- Problem-Solving Skills Are Important 90
- Management Through Team Work and Employee Involvement 90
- Problem Solving 90
  - The Problem-Solving Process 90
- Data Analysis 91
  - Frequency Tables 91
- Data Collection Frequency Table .. 91
- Percentages 92
- Pareto's 20/80 Rule 93
- Graphs 93
- Applying What You've Learned .. 95
- Creative Thinking 98
- Summary 98

©1993, JIST Works, Inc. • Indianapolis, Indiana

Chapter Ten—Ethics: Doing the Right Thing 99

What Are Ethics? 100
What Is Ethical Behavior? 101
Ethical Decision-Making Problems 101
Guidelines for Making Ethical
   Decisions 102
   Applying What You've Learned . . 103
Common Ethical Problems 103
   Applying What You've Learned . . 104
Summary 104

Chapter Eleven—Getting Ahead on the Job 105

What Concerns a New Worker . . . 106
Getting A Raise 106
   Applying What You've Learned . . 107
Getting Promoted 107
When Promotions Occur 108
   Applying What You've Learned . . 108
Career Development 109
Leaving a Job 109
   Applying What You've Learned . . 109
Summary 110

Introduction

As a supervisor and business owner I have had the opportunity to hire and fire employees over a number of years. Often employees lost these jobs due to their lack of wisdom. I fired one set of employees because their dating relationship caused problems in their work relationship. Another employee was found using drugs, and some employees just couldn't get to work.

My observations of workers being "let go" confirmed what many employers are currently voicing: entry level employees don't necessarily possess an awareness of how to keep their jobs. In other words, an employer can't assume that a new employee "knows the ropes."

Training in areas such as proper dress and hygiene, communication skills, and time management are necessary for employees to keep their positions. *Job Savvy* will help reduce the amount of time and money it takes to train new employees. Employers save money—and employees save jobs.

Job Savvy was written for two reasons:

- To help the employer keep employees on the job. As the work force shrinks, employers will find less skilled workers to do the job. Keeping a trained employee on the job will become most important.
- To help the new employee keep their new job.

In the past, it was usually up to parents to prepare their children for the responsibility of their first job. One Texan I know related this story about his first job. "My daddy said, 'Son, go down the road to old Mr. Petersen and ask him for a job.'" His father not only told him how to get the job, but also checked with Mr. Petersen to make sure that his son did the job properly. In today's society, not too many "old Mr. Petersens" exist. Close contacts with employers are rare and job training is different than in our parents' day.

©1993, JIST Works, Inc. • Indianapolis, Indiana

Problem-Solving Approach

Job Savvy contains ideas for both classroom and workshop instruction as well as individual activities. The case studies and exercises allow students to find solutions to real life work problems. The basis "how do I keep this job?" This Instructor's Guide contains suggestions for many additional activities. As the instructor or facilitator, you may choose the activities that fit the time schedule and needs of your group.

Job Savvy allows trainees to share personal experiences through group interaction. In general, I suggest that smaller groups are more effective than large groups (over 15 members) and recommend changing the group's members often. This allows sharing of more ideas from different people.

Dealing with Problem Students

I wish for you a class eagerly awaiting each session. However, realistically, not everyone in your training session will be a "happy camper." Some trainees may resent being required to complete this course. Having a sense of humor will help you deal with these "problem students." Remember, you can only act as an aid, the individual has to solve the problem.

General Lack of Interest

If a lack of interest in the course is apparent, let the trainee know you are aware of the problem. In the case of compulsory attendance, you may want to take the approach that if the individuals attempt to participate, you will attempt to make the course as rewarding as possible. As a professional, this is all you can do.

Fear of Formal Schooling

Someone in your group may have had unsuccessful experiences in formal school settings. A classroom and instructor could be very threatening to them. Placing chairs in a semi-circle, serving refreshments, and greeting individuals as they arrive will create a less threatening atmosphere. Making yourself available to trainees before class, during breaks, and after class sessions will also help breakdown some barriers and give you an idea of the groups' dynamics.

Understanding why "problem" students are the way they are will allow you to view them as individuals needing attention and direction rather than sources of irritation. A poor self-image can be a real threat to learning. As a result, they might be very shy. Involving this type of person in a small discussion group would be less threatening than a large group discussion. This person needs reassurance that they can succeed. Your facial expressions (smiling or nodding), or physical expression such as a handshake, pat on the back, or touch on the arm may act as a reward. A short comment like "great" or "good suggestion" will also give support to the individual.

The Dominating Personality

Dealing with the individual who dominates the session can be another problem. This person might be insecure. One approach might be to tell the person that others need an opportunity to contribute. If this approach doesn't prove successful, talking to the individual privately may help. If you can't solve the problem after these attempts, consider asking this person to leave.

©1993, JIST Works, Inc. • Indianapolis, Indiana

Listening is one of the invaluable skills any instructor possesses to provide insight into the trainees' needs. It is important to remember that you are in your own unique setting. You judge what approach is best in each particular situation. Use the suggestions that best meet the needs of your group. Be creative. Develop your own program.

Instructor Preparation

Begin your preparation by reading *Job Savvy* and completing the exercises to give you the student's viewpoint. (It will make you a better instructor!) *Job Savvy* was written to encourage lots of classroom participation and discussion. It is a good idea to keep notes in the margin so when one of your students gives you a real gem of an idea, you can use it in a future class.

You are the single most important element in the training session. Be enthusiastic. Your trainees will only be as interested as you are. Be positive. Emphasize the talents of the group. Compliment often. Criticize only if there is no other alternative. Do it privately if at all possible.

Remember you, the instructor, are the key to the success of this program!

Planning the First Session

As the instructor of the *Job Savvy* course, you become your students' employer. Your students should view this class as their place of employment. The **way** you conduct the class tells your students as much about the world of work as anything you **say during** the class session.

> *Note:* The words "student" and "trainee" are used interchangeably throughout this book.

Getting Prepared

Before you meet your group, there are some things you need to do for adequate preparation. These things include:

- Planning a class schedule.
- Knowing your objectives.
- Creating a comfortable physical environment.
- Preparing materials and resources.
- Developing a flexible mind-set.

©1993, JIST Works, Inc. • Indianapolis, Indiana

Planning a Class Schedule

This is a very important step in class development. A detailed agenda will enable you to keep the group moving forward to accomplish the goals you want to reach by the end of each session. Planning time slots for each session will keep slower paced students moving while keeping the interest of faster paced students. Of course, this agenda doesn't need to be written in stone. Planning ahead also allows you to prepare for outside speakers, AV presentations, and other extras to keep the class time interesting.

> *Note:* If you are working with an individual or small group, it is equally important to plan scheduled progressions. In a small setting, it is even easier to stray from the subject.

When planning your agenda it is usually wise to have some extra activities to use if time permits. The additional exercises presented are for this purpose.

Know the Class Objectives

One of the basic objectives of this training is to instill some good work habits in the student. One way to do this is to use the class as a workplace. You can accomplish this by setting some class rules and enforcing them. These rules could include:

- **Starting On Time:** Expect each trainee to be seated and ready at a set time. You might go so far as having each student "clock in."
- **Student Preparation:** Tell students what materials are needed for each session (paper, pencils, pens, etc.). (I know of a teacher who requires a shoe from any student needing to borrow a pencil. When the pencil is returned, so is the shoe.)
- **Assignment Completion:** Some type of loss or incentive system should help motivate trainees to complete their work.
- **Proper Dress:** If trainees dress in uniform, you may want to ensure they know the proper way to wear it and the acceptable standards. Likewise, students should dress in a business-like manner. Set an example by the way you dress.
- **Trainee Conduct:** Set the standards of respect in your class. This involves the way they treat themselves, fellow trainees, and you the instructor.

You will probably have other objectives for each particular class. Through class participation, the group itself may help you develop objectives that are important to them.

> *Note:* If you are working with an individual or a small group, each person could make a list of objectives. At the end of the course, these lists could be reviewed to see what has improved and what needs continued work.

Creating a Comfortable Environment

If you are unfamiliar with the surroundings, be sure to arrive early enough to check out the physical facilities. Allow time to make changes to improve the learning environment if at all possible. Some environmental influences to consider may be:

- **Room Temperature:** A room that is too hot or too cold may deter learning. As a rule a little too cool is better than too hot.
- **Adequate Lighting:** Look around for light switches. Make sure the sun isn't glaring in anyone's face.
- **Room Arrangement:** Arrange the chairs in a comfortable way. A semi-circle creates a less formal atmosphere than traditional rows. Small groups are hard to form in auditoriums. Do you want to use tables? Unless absolutely needed, tables can present barriers. If working with an individual, do you want a table or desk between you, or will you sit side by side? How will you feel most comfortable? What would make the trainee more at ease?
- **Noise Level:** If possible, make sure the room is quiet and free from other interruptions.
- **Instructor Placement:** You need to find a spot in the room to call yours. Where in the room do you feel most comfortable? Arrange the room to focus on this area. Be sure you can face the whole group as you speak. Your back should never be toward the group when you speak.

Preparing Materials and Resources

Handouts and any training aids should be organized before the class begins. A separate table may be used to organize these materials. If you have completed an agenda, you should have an idea of what you will be using. As a rule, most handouts aren't turned in after class. A handout will have more meaning if kept by the student.

If you aren't already familiar with office machines or equipment you will be using in the classroom, be sure you check them out now. Other materials such as flip charts, transparencies, and videos need to be prepared also. Using your agenda, schedule any resource people, videos, and field trips you plan to use in the sessions. Do this before the first class session to avoid scheduling conflicts later.

Developing a Flexible Mind-Set

Even with all your planning, the unexpected will happen. Prepare yourself for the unexpected. It could be positive. It could be a teachable moment. Suddenly something that has been said or done stirs minds in the class. Everyone is alert. Allow this moment to flow. Let the students continue to share. Become a learner rather than an instructor. This doesn't happen often.

The unexpected could be negative. The fire alarm accidentally goes off. The electricity goes off. The film breaks. Stay calm. Find a solution to the problem and continue the class session.

Beginning the First Session

Introducing Yourself

A simple introduction of yourself will provide an excellent beginning for the first session. Using relevant humorous events from your own experiences will make your introduction even more interesting. Your introduction could include:

- Your name
- Facts concerning your personal or family life
- A brief description of your first paying job
- Something about your educational background
- A brief description of your work history
- Your current position

Sharing this information will make you seem more human and establishes communication with the group. Since much of the work involved in this course depends on group participation, it is important that you set the example for this communication.

Introducing the Course

A brief description of your purpose and procedures for the course will give trainees an idea of what to expect. Explain rules you will enforce. Be specific. If the class begins at 8 a.m., say so. If a rest break is scheduled, tell them when and how long. (If the session is more than one hour long, a break is needed to keep everyone interested.)

Be very clear in letting trainees know exactly what responsibilities will be expected of them. Let them know how they will be made accountable for these responsibilites. Presenting these rules in a humorous way will create a less threatening atmosphere for the trainee.

Briefly go over the class agenda. If you expect any special projects to be completed by a particular date, emphasize that. In such a case, setting up dates to complete parts of the project is a good approach. In this way the student is encouraged to work on the project throughout the course.

Using word association, ask the class what comes to mind when they hear the word savvy. Write their ideas on a flip chart or overhead. As a group summarize the definition of savvy. Continue the activity by adding the term job savvy. Ask the group to list specific skills that would help a worker have job savvy in today's workplace. Conclude by pointing out that this course will aid each one of them in gaining these skills.

Introducing the Group

Divide into groups of four to five people. Ask each group to introduce themselves to each other using the following information:

- Name
- Personal or family life information
- Briefly describe your first paying job
- Briefly describe your dream job
- What you expect to gain from this course

If you list the items on a flip chart or overhead, the group can refer to it during this activity. Allow four to six minutes for each person to make their introduction. Encourage the group to ask questions. Each person must use their allotted time.

Exercises such as this, allow groups to get to know each other in a way that will encourage more class discussion in future sessions. The time spent getting to know one another will help the students feel more comfortable sharing ideas in later class activities.

Make sure students have a copy of *Job Savvy*, and read together the parable at the bottom of the introductory page under the heading "About This Book." Continue by asking the class to make a list of the possible "mosquitoes" that might cause an employee to lose their job. Encourage the group to make the list as detailed and long as possible. Ridiculous answers count.

Conclude the session by explaining any outside class assignment you may have. Remember to make these assignments meaningful. Since some trainees may already be apprehensive about a school-type atmosphere, homework could have a negative effect on them.

Additional Activity: **Real People**

The following activity exposes students to real people in the real world of work.

Interview two employers or supervisors. A supervisor is any person who gives direction to another person in a job situation. Using relatives or friends is acceptable. The interview may be done on the telephone or face-to-face. Ask this question: "What are the five most important skills you expect from a successful employee?" Have students record their answers and bring them to the next session.

Additional Activity: **Keeping a Journal**

This assignment allows students to express themselves and could be an on-going activity throughout the course.

Ask each individual to keep a *Job Savvy* journal to help them view themselves. This need only be a paragraph or two, never more than a page. For the first entry, ask them to write about their first paying job. The following questions may be used to get them thinking. It is not necessary to answer every question in the journal.

- What type of work did you do?
- How did you get the job? Who hired you?
- Did you have a supervisor or boss? What do you remember about them?
- How much pay did you receive for your work?
- How long did you keep the job?
- Why do you think you got or lost the job?

©1993, JIST Works, Inc. • Indianapolis, Indiana

Chapter One

Understanding the Employment Relationship

Chapter Purpose

> *The purpose of this chapter is to help trainees understand the employer's point of view in the job world. The trainee will also learn about employee rights and employer's responsibilities.*

©1993, JIST Works, Inc. • Indianapolis, Indiana

A new job is a real adventure. Each employee has expectations of what the job will provide. Observing my own sons confirms the many expectations an employee may have:

My boys took over a newspaper route that had been without a regular carrier for several months. The agreement with the newspaper was that they could keep any overdue bills they could collect. This led the boys to envision large amounts of money accumulating in their bank accounts which made them very persistent in their pursuit of the overdue charges. Money was their great expectation. They gave no thought to the fact that their employer wasn't requiring any money for the actual newspapers that had been delivered.

Most employees are like my sons. They expect the job to provide for their satisfaction. The employer's expectations aren't considered. While most employees know that their employer has responsibilities, they are unaware of what those responsibilities are. Often employees have an unrealistic understanding of their employer's expectations.

What Does My Employer Want Anyway?

Allow time for the students to read and do this exercise. Discuss the seven basic skills comparing answers to question #2 with those found in the "Workplace Basics" study.

Additional Activity: Interviewing Employers or Supervisors

If you used the employer/supervisor interviews assignment in the previous session, divide into groups of four to five people. Each group should select a person to record results. Ask each group member to tell what skills the employers and supervisors they interviewed expected. The recorder lists these skills, keeping a tally of any duplications. (The group decides on duplications.) Allow 10 to 15 minutes for this activity.

Have the groups come together. Each recorder should read their group list and tally. Place the consolidated list on a flip-chart or overhead. Again, keep a tally of duplications allowing the class to make these determinations.

Looking over the list, ask the class to point out any skills that might be an unreasonable employer or supervisor expectation. Discuss these unreasonable expectations if they exist. Allow free expression of opinions as to the fairness or unfairness of the expectation. No consensus need be drawn.

As a group, find the five most frequently listed skills. Compare this list with the "Workplace Basics" study. How do the local employers' expectations compare to the survey? If there is a difference, can it be explained in any way?

Dependability vs. Reliability

Before doing the next two exercises in *Job Savvy*, discuss the slight difference in the meaning of dependability and reliability. (See box in student workbook.) How could a dependable employee be unreliable? How could the opposite be true? Which skill is more valuable: dependability or reliability?

Have each individual fill in the "Employee Skills Checklist." Using the checklist, tally the group's opinion from most important to least important.

Introduce the next exercise on the same page. Provide time for individual group members to complete the exercise. Then as a group, discuss the importance of each skill to an organization.

Employer Expectations

Have the group read the section entitled "Business Basics." Point out the information in the box "Profit." Discuss each of the three points under "Business Basics."

Have the group read the section called "Employee Skills." Briefly discuss the 10 self-management skills in the box. Be sure the group understands the meaning of each skill.

Additional Activity: Products and Services

Have the group list the various places they have worked. Compile a list of products or services represented. (If you used the employer/supervisor survey assignment suggested in the first session activities, compile a list of products and services represented by the survey.) This should provide the group with a basic idea of the types of businesses in your community. After compiling the list, consider the following questions.

- What might affect the quality of these products or services?
- What rules might the employer or supervisor enforce to maintain this quality?

Additional Activity: Satisfy the Customer's Needs and Wants

Divide into groups of three to four people. Ask each group to write a short skit involving customers and employees serving the public. This can be any type of business from a drug store to a restaurant. It may include both poor and good service. Encourage the groups to be as creative as possible. They may even create props and costumes. Allow time for the groups to plan their skits during this session.

Have each group present their skit to the whole group. Ask the other groups to list the types of good and poor service they observe during the skits. Discuss customer's feelings due to the type of service they received.

Exercise: Journal Assignment

Ask groups to patronize three different businesses in town. Have students record their reactions, both positive and negative, as "customers". Have them analyze the reasons for their feelings in their journals. What did an employee do to cause their reaction?

Additional Activity: Make a Profit

To help students understand profit and expenses, use the following case study. Divide into small groups to work out the solution.

You are in charge of a 6-week summer swim program for pre-school children. This is a profit-making venture.

- List all the expenses that might possibly be involved in your business.
- How many employees will you need? What salaries will you pay them?
- How much will you charge each student?
- What factors other than the expenses you listed may affect your profit?

Additional Activity: Production Expenses

Have the group form a business such as making cookies, candy, or peanut butter sandwiches. The group must list all the production expenses. Have the class calculate how much of their product must be sold in order to buy pizza for the entire group. Sell the product. Have the group record sales. Remember pizza for everyone if the profit is great enough, or bread and water if it isn't.

Additional Activity: Increasing Trainee Awareness

If you are training employees for your specific company, use your company's products or services for this activity. With the trainees, go through the process of making this product. Together list the expenses the company must incur. Help trainees become aware of the hidden expenses that business pay. Many employees are totally unaware that expenses such as electricity, insurance, heating, and cooling are a part of a business' expenses.

Exercise: Journal Assignment

Ask individuals to choose a self-management skill they could improve and write a plan to improve this skill.

Applying What You've Learned

Have each individual do Case Study 1 and 2. Using the case studies, have members of the group play the roles of Tom and his supervisor Janet, and Angel and her supervisor. The rest of the group observes the supervisor's response to each situation. Have the groups complete these statements and then have them explain the reasons for reacting this way.

- If I were the boss, I would have done . . .

  _____
  _____
  _____

- If I were the boss, I would have done . . .

  _____
  _____
  _____

What Should You Expect?

Have each individual fill in the columns. Give the group time to complete their answers. As a group make a list of the reasons people work. Post the list for further reference.

Next list things people like and dislike about their jobs. Finally compile a list of employee expectations and wants. Post these lists for reference.

Reasons for Working

Have the group read "Reasons for Working." Look at the first information box. Compare the reason given for working in this poll with the group's list. Circle the corresponding reasons.

Look at the second information box. Compare this information with the group's second list. Briefly discuss what an employee can do if they don't like their job. Remind the group that no job is perfect all the time.

Ad*ditional Activity:* **Video Presentation**

Show the video *Why Work?* with Dean Curtis, a trainer who works with unemployed persons. This 15-minute video presents six reasons for being employed. It is a catalog product available through JIST Works, Inc.

Understanding Your Rights

Have students read and fill out this section together. This is probably the most complex part of the book. It is important that employees understand their rights according to the law.

As the instructor, you will need to be aware of the laws in your particular state. Because federal and state laws constantly change, I have provided only a review of these laws. As the instructor, you will need to make the decision as to what additional information your group needs. The reference list at the end of chapter 1 will help you in further research. Local agencies in your particular area such as OSHA, the Equal Opportunity Commission, and the State Department of Labor are another means of information.

Additional Activity: **Researching the Laws**

This activity divides the large group into small research groups. Each group is assigned a different set of laws to research for class presentation. Provide time to allow the groups to meet and gather information from the library or other sources. (If library facilities aren't available, you should provide packets of information on each subject to complete this activity.) Using these packets of current information and the material in *Job Savvy*, each research group should make their presentation to the entire class.

The division of the laws could be: fair wage, equal opportunity, child labor laws, worker safety, labor relations, and fair treatment.

Additional Activity: Mock Trial

Stage a "mock trial." Create a scene of an employer vs. an employee and allow the class to conduct the trial. The judge should be in charge of the proceedings. The charges should involve misconduct on the part of the employer. (A case involving a just cause for dismissal would be a possible suggestion.) The court should include lawyers for both clients, witnesses, and a jury. Other members of the court may be added for interest. The jury may be allowed to actually bring in a verdict.

Following the trial, discuss the practicality of bringing such actions to court.

Additional Activity: Guest Speaker

Using community resources expose trainees to the real world. Suggestions for resource people involved in the laws dealing with employee rights are: a union leader or representative, a lawyer, or a local business employer.

Before the resource person speaks to the group, a list of questions could be prepared as an individual or group project.

Resolving Employee Rights Issues

Have the group read this section and discuss the best way to deal with a problem.

Additional Activity: Resolutions to Rights Issues

Divide into groups of three or four. Discuss the following situations. Ask individuals how they would react if they were the employee. Each group should decide the best way to resolve the problem. Share the solutions with the entire group.

Situation 1

Ty is 15 years old and works in the diner at a 24-hour truck stop. Last Thursday the late night waitress suddenly got ill and couldn't come to work. Ty's manager asked him to work till 2 a.m. Ty had already worked his usual shift.

Situation 2

Mike and Ann began and ended training on the same day. They started work on the same day as tellers at the Old Standard Bank. They each work five 8-hour days each week. In fact, they often work in adjoining teller desks.

Today was their first payday. To celebrate, they had lunch together. Over lunch, they compared paychecks. Much to their surprise, Mike's check was $100 more than Ann's.

Situation 3

Starr works in a photo processing plant. Recently she developed a rash on her arms. Her doctor says it was caused by a chemical. Starr suspects she has come in contact with the chemical in her work situation. She has never received any instructions concerning chemicals in the photo processing lab.

Situation 4

Barth works at the Sleepy Bye Mattress Company. After working six months, he has expressed an interest in joining the Local 82 of the Bed Makers' Union. Today his foreman called him into the office area, and pleasantly told Barth that the company's owner really doesn't approve of the union.

Applying What You've Learned

Allow time for the group to complete this exercise. Using the two case studies, discuss the fact that all jobs involve both likes and dislikes. This will vary from person to person, because of individual differences.

Exercise: Journal Assignment

Have the group write two or three paragraphs using the following opening sentence:

"If I believed my boss was treating me unfairly, I would . . . ."

Summary

Review this chapter by discussing the three concepts involved in the employer-employee realationship. Questions for discussion are:

- Why is an employer in business?
- Why do you as an employee want to work?
- What do you find satisfying about your work?
- What should the relationship between an employer and an employee be based upon? How is this shown by the employer? By the employee?

Chapter Two
Your First Day on the Job

Chapter Purpose

> *The purpose of this chapter is to acquaint the student with the normal occurrences of the first day at a new job.*

First impressions last a long time. So the first day on the job is very important to the new worker. Yet at a time when the new employee wants to make the very best impression, an awkwardness sets in and problems can very easily arise.

Remember your first day on the new job? Rolling and tossing the night before? Asking someone if you looked OK as you prepared to leave the house? Arriving at your new place of employment madly looking for a parking place hoping you wouldn't be late? All this and more awaits your trainees on their first day.

©1993, JIST Works, Inc. • Indianapolis, Indiana

While I can't reserve them a parking space right in front of the building, together we can offer them some information to help prevent some embarrassing first-day moments. I will provide information on payroll deductions required by the government as well as various fringe benefits offered by employers. Many new workers have no knowledge of payroll deductions. In such cases, the first payroll check can be a great disappointment.

> *Note: The procedures described in this chapter are generally used by companies. If you are training for a particular business organization, you may introduce their procedures to the group.*

Reporting to Work

Read the introduction to chapter 2 of *Job Savvy* including the section "Reporting to Work."

Additional Activity: Ice Breaker

Have the trainees complete this sentence then share competed sentences with the group.

"Today is your first day on the new job. Last night you had a nightmare. You dreamed that you arrived at work and you . . . ."

Dress Appropriately

Have students continue reading and filling out the exercises. Allow time for students to share information on the type of clothing needed in their job.

> *Note: If you are training for a particular organization, point out what dress requirements that business has.*
>
> *Suggestion: If the trainees don't have jobs, you may assign imaginary jobs to them. Write various jobs on index cards and randomly hand them out to individuals in the group. This will give trainees a basis to answer questions in Job Savvy.*

Starting the Day

Have each student read this section and fill in the information. (The student may use a current or imaginary job when filling in the information.) Have them attempt to answer as many of the questions as they can. Then as a group discuss this information and the possible answers.

> *Note: This exercise will give you some idea of the understanding the group has concerning first day procedures.*

Read and discuss the information given under "Orientation" and "Personnel Information."

Additional Activity: **Required Documentation**

Ask each individual to bring the required documents in the "Paperwork Checklist" to class. Look over the documents. Discuss the information the employer would need from each document.

Applying What You've Learned

Give individuals time to read and work through the case studies. As a group, discuss the questions.

Payroll Information and Enrollment

It is important for trainees to understand the information in this section. Because it is somewhat involved, you may want to discuss only part of it and break before continuing with the rest.

Additional Activity: **Reference Groups**

Divide into groups of three to four trainees. Assign a different topic to each group. Have the group collect the information on their assigned topics and present it to the entire group. (You may wish to compile a file of information on each subject for the groups' reference. This might depend on the type library facilities available to you.) Discussion and questions should follow each presentation. Suggested topics are: withholding taxes, payroll information, fringe benefits, required benefits, voluntary deductions, and employee services.

Applying What You've Learned

Be sure the trainees fill out the forms in this section. Go through these together to make sure everyone understands their format. Discuss the various fringe benefits. Be sure to point out that not all of these benefits are available through all employers. Stress the two rules of thumb for choosing fringe benefits found on page 30.

©1993, JIST Works, Inc. • Indianapolis, Indiana

Fringe Benefits

Discuss the meaning of a "cafeteria" plan. (See box under "Fringe Benefits" on page 29.) Continue discussing the benefits listed under "Paid Time Off," "Required Benefits," and "Voluntary Deductions." Continue with the section on "Employee Services."

Have each individual complete "Selecting Benefits and Deductions." Divide into small groups. Have each person share reasons they would or wouldn't choose a particular benefit or deduction.

After the discussion ends, ask each group to continue with the next section "Other Employer-Provided Benefits." Have each person select the benefits they believe are important and share the reasons with the group.

> *Note: If you are training for a particular organization, you may point out the fringe benefits the company offers their employees.*

Applying What You've Learned

In the large group, have each trainee read the case studies and list the benefits that each of these individuals needs. Discuss the two situations.

Additional Activity: Guest Speaker

A community resource person could help explain much of this material. Contact a personnel manager, a state or private employment agent, or a company trainer willing to speak to the trainees. To encourage better listening ask the group to submit questions for the speaker to answer.

Introduction to the Job

Have the group read this entire section. Discuss the material covered using the following questions.

Work Instructions

- What is the supervisor's responsibility on your first day on the job?
- Why is it important to ask questions when instructions are given?
- How can you know what your supervisor expects of you?

Supplies and Equipment

- What would a new worker need to know about supplies and equipment?
- Is there anyone in the group who could share information from a work experience involving supplies and equipment?
- Why is it important to the organization that an employee know the rules about supplies and equipment?

©1993, JIST Works, Inc. • Indianapolis, Indiana

Telephone System
- What might a new worker need to know about the telephone system?
- Why is this skill important to the company?
- Could anyone in the group share their experiences with a telephone system in the workplace?

Breaks
- What does a new worker need to know about breaks?
- What are the reasons for taking breaks?
- Is there anyone in the group who could share information on taking breaks in their individual work situation?

Additional Activity: **Facility Tour**

If you are training for a particular organization or company, a brief tour of the facility would be appropriate as an introduction to the trainees. Explain the company's policy concerning supplies and equipment, the telephone, and breaks.

Off to a Good Start

Together read and discuss "Off to a Good Start." Go through "Tips for Adjustment to the New Job." Sharing some of your own experiences as a new worker will add a more personal touch to the discussion. Emphasize the following important thoughts to the group.

- **Be positive:** New workers often feel ill-at-ease. How can you approach a new job in a positive manner?
- **Ask for help:** New workers need to realize that no question is foolish. Supervisors expect questions.
- **Have a good sense of humor:** Prepare your trainees to expect some teasing. As they establish themselves in the group, this treatment should disappear. (Excessive abuse needs to be reported to the supervisor.)
- **Find a buddy:** Emphasize that a "buddy" should be someone who knows about the job and is willing to help. Not every worker will meet those qualifications.
- **Follow instructions:** Remind the trainees in order to follow instructions, they must listen carefully to the supervisor. Questions may need to be asked, but repeating the same questions will irritate a supervisor. A new worker needs to listen carefully and follow through on instructions.
- **Read the company policies:** If you are training for a particular organization, this would be an excellent time to present the company's policies to the trainees. Point out that the supervisor will expect the employee to read these policies and ask questions if needed.

Applying What You've Learned

Give time for each individual to do "Applying What You've Learned." Divide into small groups. Ask each group to share their response to the two case studies.

Summary

Conclude the chapter by reading the summary. Use the following discussion question to summarize this chapter.

- What can you do to make your first day on the job go smoother?

Chapter Three
Making a Good Impression

CHAPTER PURPOSE

> *The purpose of this chapter is to make the trainees aware of making a good impression on the job. The chapter discusses dressing appropriately for various types of work. It deals with personal hygiene and unpleasant mannerisms.*

©1993, JIST Works, Inc. • Indianapolis, Indiana

He wore bib overalls and a plaid flannel shirt. His hair was messy, his beard long and disheveled. In fact, he didn't even smell too great. The new car salesperson just happened to NOT have any other customers that afternoon or the ragged man would have been ignored.

Approaching the man, the salesperson asked, "May I help you today?"

"Well, yes, you can! I'll take that blue Cadillac over in the corner."

Following this statement the man pulled out a wad of thousand dollar bills from his pocket. The cash sale quickly took place, or so goes the tale of the miser from my hometown.

Looks can be deceiving. However, in today's society one's outward appearance has an effect on the way others react to us. We are all judged on appearance, personal hygiene, and mannerisms.

> *Note: Several of the subjects in this chapter could be sensitive issues, such as body odor, weight, and acne. As the instructor, you need to approach these subjects as understandingly as possible. If someone in the group has a special problem, you may wish to talk to them privately.*

Wearing the Right Clothes

Have the group read the introduction and section, "Wearing the Right Clothes." When introducing this chapter emphasize that the subject isn't natural beauty. Neatness and appropriate dress makes everyone more attractive.

Dress Codes

Discuss the meaning of an official dress code. Ask individuals in the group to share their experiences with dress codes. Have them answer the following questions:

- What were the restrictions?
- How was the code enforced?
- Who enforced the code?

Be sure the group understands that an official dress code must be fair. It applies to all persons working in that situation. A dress code is a written rule.

> *Note: If you are training for a particular organization, you may introduce that company's dress code to the trainees.*

Discuss the meaning of an unofficial dress code. The following questions may be used to stimulate conversation.

- How can a new employee know what the unofficial dress code is?
- Why is it important for a new employee to know about an unofficial dress code?

- How can an unofficial dress code affect a supervisor's opinion of a worker?
- Is an unofficial dress code always fair?
- What effect could the unofficial dress code have on one's job advancement?

Appropriate Dress

Don't assume your trainees know what is appropriate dress for different type jobs. In today's society, people tend to dress for comfort. Younger people are easily influenced by peers and current styles when choosing their clothing.

Even adults don't always know how to dress. I was recently at a patio buffet. The invitation read "Cool and Casual Dress." The style of dress actually ranged from shorts and jeans to dresses and heels. Knowing how to dress appropriately isn't always easy.

Be specific as you discuss this topic. Opinions may vary from region to region. Have an understanding of what is appropriate in your particular area.

Additional Activity: Clothes Closet

Bring a suitcase of assorted clothing to class. Take one article of clothing out of the suitcase at a time. Have the class brainstorm what jobs might require this type of clothing. Write their suggestions on a flip chart or overhead projector. Examples of clothing are jeans, sneakers, high heels, tie, suit, sport jacket, bathing suit, shorts, and work shoes.

Neat Dress

Be sure that the group knows that neatness does count in the work world. With torn jeans being the current style, there is a need to point out the "correct" clothing for the job. The subject of shoes also needs to be addressed. Discuss the fact that some businesses require their employees to wear leather shoes or safety shoes as opposed to sneakers. Wearing comfortable shoes on the job is important for the worker.

Additional Activity: Fashion Show

Have each student dress for a particular job. Some students may dress inappropriately. Discuss what is right or wrong about the way they are dressed for their work.

> *Variation:* Have an occupational dress up session. Assign various job titles to each student. The student must dress for that particular job.

Additional Activity: Color Analysis

Ask a color co-ordination expert or a home economist to discuss dress with the group. Ways to inexpensively stretch the working person's wardrobe would be helpful.

Uniforms

As a group, brainstorm various occupations that require uniforms. List the ideas on a flip chart or the overhead. Discuss the reasons some businesses require their employees to wear uniforms.

Ask anyone in the group, who has worked in a business and was required to wear a uniform to share their knowledge. Use the questions on uniforms under "Wearing the Right Clothes" to guide this discussion.

Additional Activity: Slide Show

Develop a set of slides showing various uniforms. As you go through the slides, discuss the occupation represented by each uniform. The slides could involve people in your own community (the postman, an EMT, a local police officer, a fast food server, a waitress, a security guard, etc.).

> *Note: If you are training for a particular organization, you should explain the company's policy about uniforms. Answer the questions about uniforms listed in* Job Savvy. *You or someone in the group could model a uniform. Show the proper way to wear it.*

Safety Clothing

Discuss the fact that some clothing is worn for protection. Ask the following questions.

- Why would it be unwise for an assembly line worker to wear a long chain?
- What would be a good safety precaution for long hair in a job involving machinery?
- Why are steel-toed shoes necessary for some workers? What types of jobs might require this type of shoe? (If you have steel-toed shoes, these could be shown to the group.)
- In what type jobs would leather shoes rather than sneakers be better protection?

Special Safety Equipment

Have the group read the information on special safety equipment. Go through the listed safety equipment in *Job Savvy*. Discuss what each item is and its use.

Additional Activity: Safety First

Have available various types of safety equipment for the trainees to see. Demonstrate how the equipment is used and why it is needed.

- Using a pumpkin as a "head:" place a hard hat on it. Drop a bowling ball or large rock on the hard hat. Repeat the activity without the hard hat. Compare the results.

- **Use a moving machine such as an electric fan:** Use yarn to show what could happen if hair or a chain were caught in the machine.

> *Note:* If you are training for a particular company, demonstrate any safety equipment required for the job.

Additional Activity: **Guest Speaker**

Ask an industrial nurse or a safety expert to talk to the group about safety on the job.

Applying What You've Learned

Allow time for each individual to do the exercises. Divide into small groups of three to four members. Have each group discuss their selections and the reasons for each choice.

Exercise: **Journal Assignment**

Have each student choose a particular job. Write a description of the appropriate dress for this job. Give reasons for this type of clothing.

Positive Grooming

Introduce this section by stating this is private information. It won't be shared with the group. Allow each individual time to fill in the information in this section.

Good Grooming Habits

With the group, go through the checklist under "Good Grooming Habits." After the discussion, give the group time to fill out the checklist individually.

Additional Activity: **Cosmetic Demonstration**

Ask a makeup expert or a hair stylist to demonstrate appropriate hair styles and makeup for the workplace.

Read the following and discuss the problems this might cause in the workplace.

> *Note:* "A Word About Cologne: Moderation."

Special Hygiene Concerns

Have the group read this section. Discuss each of the good health practices listed.

> *Note: If you are training for a particular organization, point out any special hygiene practices necessary for the job.*

Additional Activity: Guest Speaker

Ask a local health department employee to share state and local laws concerning hygiene practices in public places.

Special Personal Considerations

Have the group read this section. Discuss each of the conditions and what effect they might have in the workplace.

Additional Activity: Guest Speaker

Any of the following specialists might be helpful in dealing with these topics of consideration: a physical practicioner, a weight loss expert, a personal trainer, or a dermatologist.

> *Note: If you are training for a particular organization, the company may have a physical conditioning facility available to employees. The group could visit this facility as a field trip.*

Additional Activity: Physical Fitness

Challenge the group to plan a physical activity program for themselves. It need not be complicated. Simply taking a 30 minute walk each day would be healthy. Choosing an enjoyable activity is also important. This will make sticking to the program less tedious. Ask the group to attempt a physical activity three times each week. Challenge them to keep at the activity for at least a month.

Mannerisms

Be sure the group understands the meaning of mannerisms. Go through the list of unpleasant mannerisms. List other mannerisms that people sometime unconsciously use.

Additional Activity: Irritating Mannerisms

Introduce this topic as "a gum chewing, picking and pulling, slang-using" instructor. Exaggerating these and other irritating mannerisms during your presentation will make the group aware of the meaning of mannerisms. Ask for trainees to demonstrate any other annoying mannerisms.

Exercise: Journal Assignment

Ask each individual to write about an irritating mannerism or speech habit they have. A relative or friend can help them identify one if they can't think of one. Have them plan a way to overcome this habit. Recording it in their journal will help them remember to improve in this area.

Additional Activity: Guest Speaker

Ask a speech therapist or speech teacher to address the group about developing good speech habits and overcoming speech problems.

Applying What You've Learned

Have the group complete the two case studies. Together discuss the questions and the reasons for each answer.

Summary

Read the chapter summary. In reviewing the chapter, ask the following questions.

- Why is proper dress in the workplace important to you?
- What effect does good personal hygiene have in the workplace?

Chapter Four

Punctuality and Attendance[1]

CHAPTER PURPOSE

> *The purpose of this chapter is to help students understand that being dependable is important. The problems created by an undependable worker and the effects of absenteeism are presented. Since absenteeism is one of the major reasons for firing employees, a new worker needs to understand that a good attendance record is important in keeping a job. Problems that may cause absenteeism and suggestions for overcoming these problems are given.*

---

1 Note: You may want to go directly to the additional activity "Late Arrival" before introducing this topic.

©1993, JIST Works, Inc. • Indianapolis, Indiana

Grasping the concept of time is sometimes difficult for the young. My youngest son often wanted to know how long he had to wait before we would leave for a special family outing. It was frustrating to me that terms like 15 or 30 minutes meant nothing to him. Finally we solved the time problem by relating it to "Sesame Street" or a shorter program for a lesser amount of time. In that way he had an idea of when to be ready to go.

Like my son, many young workers seem to lack an ability to schedule their time. An alarm clock and a calendar aren't a part of their lives. Getting to work on time isn't a high priority. They don't usually plan ahead for that unexpected occurrence.

Additional Activity: Late Arrival

Arrive in the room 5 to 10 minutes late. (This will be most effective if you have been starting the group at a rigid time.) Offer all types of excuses for your late arrival. (Flat tire, the cows got out, the alarm didn't go off, your mother called, etc.)

Ask the group to share their feelings when you didn't arrive on time. What problems, if any, did it cause?

Problems Caused by Absenteeism and Tardiness

Ask the group to define absenteeism and tardiness. Write their definitions on a flip chart or the overhead. Point out that both can cause problems in the workplace.

Additional Activity: Teamwork Game

Divide into groups of five or six players. Have each team sit in a circle. Give each group a skein of yarn or a roll of kite string. The object of the game is to put the yarn or string into a ball. This is a team effort.

One person starts. At a given signal, the first player starts. (Allow 15-30 seconds for each player to work.) Play continues by passing the yarn or string to the player on the left. Continue the activity by signaling a player change every 15 to 30 seconds. The first team to have a ball or yarn or string wins. You may want to provide a special treat to inspire the competition.

> *Note: Prior to class, make arrangements with a few students to act as "undependable" players. These individuals may leave the group when their turn arrives. They may sit and talk to someone while they are supposed to be working. They may drop the ball or simply stop. At the end of the game, discuss how the other members of the teams felt about these players. (You may want to provide a treat for everyone to protect the undependable people!)*

Have individuals complete the exercise. Divide into small groups to discuss the situation. Have the groups consider these additional questions.

- If you were one of Lee's co-workers, how would you react to Lee when he returned to work?
- If George ignores the situation, how do you think Lee will react?
- If you were George, how would you handle this situation?

Using the material in *Job Savvy* and students' own ideas, have the group examine and list the problems created by undependable employees. Use the following headings on a chalkboard or flipchart to aid the discussion.

Effects of Absenteeism on:
- Employer
- Supervisor
- Co-workers
- Employee

Be sure to highlight the information in the "Customer Satisfaction" box. Why are dependable workers needed to provide good customer service?

> *Note: If you are training for a particular organization, you should present the company's policy concerning absenteeism and tardiness.*

What's Your Excuse?

Ask each individual to fill in this table. Point out the fact that some of the listed items may be valid excuses, but solutions are needed to avoid the problem.

Additional Activity: No More Excuses

Allow the trainees to share their list with one other person. (Let them find a friend since this may be private information.) Together let them answer these questions:

- What is my weakness in this area?
- How can I solve this problem?

How Lifestyle Affects Your Work

Discuss each of the areas listed here. It is possible that trainees believe some of these areas aren't their employer's concern. Openly discuss their feelings.

Point out that an employer may not control an employee's personal life; however, an employer may be influenced as a result of some of these items. Consequently a worker's promotions and continued employment may be affected by them.

Additional Activity: Solving Problems

Use the following worksheet dealing with lifestyle and work. Divide into small groups. Using the information in this section, have each group find a solution to each problem.

In the blank box, (problem number 5) ask each group to create a problem and find a solution. After completing the worksheet, each group should present their original problem to the entire class and challenge them to find a solution.

PROBLEM	SOLUTION
1. A mechanic goes home late each evening, barely stopping work long enough to eat, then works on cars until bedtime.	
2. A worker lacks energy, so much so, the work doesn't get finished.	
3. A worker ignores a customer while talking to a co-worker of the opposite sex.	
4. An employee is late this morning with this excuse, "My best friend was arrested in a drug bust last night."	
5. (Create a problem)	

©1993, JIST Works, Inc. • Indianapolis, Indiana

Your Lifestyle and Stress

Have each individual fill out the stress chart and rate themselves.

Additional Activity: Stress Dots

Pass out stress dots to the group. These are small dots, which change color to reflect the individual's emotional state. Ask the group to wear the stress dots for a day. Keep an hourly record. What color was the stress dot? What were you doing at the time?

> *Note:* For more information write, BioDots International, Inc., P.O. Box 2246, Indianapolis, IN 46206, or call 1-800-272-2340.

Exercise: Journal Assignment

Ask the group to record something that makes them feel stress Have them answer the following questions to guide their writing. Is there a way to avoid this stress? What activity eases your feelings of stress? If the group is willing, this would be an excellent journal article to share.

Planning to Get to Work

This section deals with five steps that can help an employee maintain a good job attendance record. It is important to go over each step. These are steps to take before an emergency arrives. This should be emphasized since new workers don't usually plan ahead. Read through this section together. Discuss each of these areas.

1. **Reliable Transportation:** Have the group list the public transportation available in your area. How do you get a taxi? How do you read a bus schedule? If the group hasn't used bus transportation, taking a bus ride as a field trip would be helpful.

Additional Activity: Guest Speaker

Ask an auto mechanic to share ways to maintain a car for reliable transportation.

2. **Reliable Child Care:** Discuss the need for reliable child care and the problems caused if arrangements aren't made beforehand. Have the group use the Yellow Pages to find available child care centers and health care programs. Assign trainees to call some of these centers to find out information such as:
   - What activities are available?
   - What are the child care hours?
   - Is the center closed during holidays or bad weather?
   - What happens when a child is ill?
   - What arrangements can be made if a child can not be picked up at the usual time?

Additional Activity: **Guest Speaker**

Ask a day care director to share information with the group. Have the group prepare questions before the session. This will help them know what to ask a day care center they may want to use.

3. **Use a Calendar:** Use the calendar forms in *Job Savvy* to have the trainees practice using a calendar. The book presents both a weekly and a monthly calendar format. Encourage the group to fill in both business and personal schedules. Point out that each influences the other.

Additional Activity: **Guest Speaker**

A time management expert or a video on time management could provide additional information in this area.

4. **Plan a Schedule with Your Supervisor:** Discuss the following questions. How much should a supervisor know about your personal life? Why is it important for a supervisor to know about your personal plans? Have the trainees ask their supervisors how far in advance they make their schedules. How much notice is needed for a 5-day vacation? How much notice is needed for a one-day appointment? Is it possible to take a half day off? Have the group share this information.

5. **Call the Employer:** Discuss the information a supervisor needs to know when you can't be at work. Who should you talk to if your supervisor isn't there? Each person should ask their supervisors how many days in a year is considered reasonable to be absent from work. What disciplinary action is taken, when absences are excessive?

Notifying Your Supervisor

Discuss the following question. What is the proper procedure to follow when notifying a supervisor of a delay or absence from work?

Additional Activity: **Role Play**

Have trainees pair up. One member will be the supervisor. The other is the employee calling to tell the supervisor why they can't be at work. You may assign the reasons or have the trainees make them up.

Applying What You've Learned

Have each individual fill out this checklist. Go over the list and discuss whether the reasons are good or bad and why.

> *Note: Highlight the material in the "Friday/Monday Syndrome" box.*

Getting to Work on Time

Read the material and discuss each point. Emphasize again the importance of planning ahead and allowing time for unexpected emergencies.

Exercise: Journal Assignment

Ask the group to describe something in their lifestyle that prevents them from being a dependable worker. Then have them answer this question, "How can I change my lifestyle to make myself more dependable?"

Applying What You've Learned

Give the group time to complete the case studies. Go over the case studies and questions together.

Summary

Read the chapter summary. Discuss the value of dependability using the following questions.

- How will a business benefit by having dependable employees?
- How will an employee benefit by having good attendance and being punctual?

Chapter Five
Learning to Do Your Job

CHAPTER PURPOSE

> *The purpose of this chapter is to help trainees realize learning is a continual process. Trying a new recipe, following directions to a new restaurant, and putting a tricycle together are all learning projects. Learning takes place by reading books and magazines, watching other people, and sharing information.*

Not everyone learns in the same manner. Throughout this chapter, trainees are encouraged to find their own learning style. This enables them to learn at their maximum capacity.

This chapter also deals with the fact that continued learning is essential to improving job skills to qualify for advancement on the job. An employer will be impressed with a worker that is seeking to improve his skills.

When did you begin learning? At age 5 when you entered kindergarten and learned all you ever really needed to know about life? Of course not! When will your quest for knowledge end? With a bachelor's degree, or a master's degree? Would a Ph.D. complete your learning? Of course not! Learning is a constant, continuing process. Pick up a magazine, turn on the television, watch a demonstration, or talk with a friend—learning will take place.

For many people, however, learning is viewed as a formal structured activity controlled by others within the confines of four classroom walls. It is viewed as a completed task. Graduation means an end to learning, a task completed. (However, this ignores the fact that the graduation ceremony is really called "commencement," meaning beginning.)

Thinking About Learning

Read together the chapter introduction. It is important for trainees to realize that learning is a continuous activity. Learning takes place throughout one's entire life. Employers expect their employees to continue learning on the job.

Discuss the learning that takes place in the first five years of a child's life. Make a list of the basics a child learns. Discuss how this learning takes place. Point out that much of this learning takes place in an unstructured, learning environment. Much of this learning is done by observing and doing.

Make a list of learning experiences the group has had outside the formal classroom. What was learned? How was it learned? Who or what served as the "instructor?"

> *Note: Get excited about these learning experiences. Some people in the group may believe they are no longer capable of learning. Others have experienced failure in the structured classroom. These people have a special need for praise in their informal learning. They need to know that this learning is as valuable as classroom learning.*

Have each individual read and do the exercise, "Thinking About Learning," and share their learning project with another trainee. This activity may be continued by combining two groups and allowing more people to interact.

Additional Activity: Continued Learning

Divide into small groups. Ask each group to consider facts about an automobile. Have them make a list about how and what people of different ages learn about automobiles. What would be essential for a child to know about an automobile? What learning would be necessary for a teenager? What learning would be important for an adult to know? Give each group a chart to fill out with the headings "Children," "Teenagers," and "Adults." Share ideas together when the groups have completed the task.

Additional Activity: Structured vs. Unstructured Learning

To introduce the idea of structured and unstructured learning brainstorm as a large group. Make a list of formal learning institutions. Make a list of informal learning experiences available. Discuss the ways that informal learning might take place in these settings.

Additional Activity: Updating Skills

To introduce the need for updating one's skills, ask the group to brainstorm a list of all the equipment that might be found in an office. Circle the equipment that would have been found in this same office 20 years ago. Point out the technical changes that have taken place over the years.

Learning How to Do Your Job

Discuss the need for workers to know what is expected of them on the job. Have the group read and fill out this exercise. Discuss these lists and the reasons for putting the various items on the list.

Where to Find Information About Your Job

Have the group read this section. Together go through the list of job information.

Job Descriptions

Discuss what a job description is. Make sure trainees understand that additional information may be needed to have a full idea of one's job responsibilities.

> *Note: If you are training for a particular organization, go through the company's job description with the trainees. If no job description exists, write a job description together.*

Additional Activity: What's My Job?

Divide into groups of two. Give each group a specific and different job. No group should tell another group what their job is. Have each group write out a job description. To help students understand what is included in a job description, go over the following job description as an example to use as a guide. When the activity is completed, have each group read their description. The other groups should try to guess what job they are describing.

> *Note: You may wish to list the various jobs on the overhead or a flip chart to make this an easier assignment.*

©1993, JIST Works, Inc. • Indianapolis, Indiana

Example of a Job Description

CLERK

Reports to: Project Director   *Supervises:* No one

Qualifications Desired:

- Typing speed of 55 words/minute
- Ability to take shorthand
- Secretarial, receptionist, and/or file clerk experience
- Ability to follow directions closely
- Ability to systematically file clients' records
- Ability to communicate well and interact with others

Duties and Responsibilities:

- Type staff correspondence
- Pick up and distribution of incoming mail
- Type all reports, budgets, forms, and other project materials
- Mail outgoing correspondence and packages
- Operate office machines as required
- Take meeting notes for staff projects
- Maintain correspondence and general files
- Answer the telephone and direct calls to the proper staff
- Take phone messages
- Maintain accurate records
- Update files weekly
- Attend all staff meetings

JOB DESCRIPTION WORKSHEET

JOB TITLE: _____

Reports to: _____   Supervises: _____

Qualifications Desired: *Duties and Responsibilities:*

_____   _____
_____   _____
_____   _____
_____   _____
_____   _____
_____   _____
_____   _____
_____   _____

©1993, JIST Works, Inc. • Indianapolis, Indiana

Training

Discuss the two types of training that prepares new employees for their job. Ask group members to share experiences they have had in their work.

> *Note: If you are training for a particular organization, tell the group what type of training they will be experiencing in preparation for their job.*

Exercise: Journal Assignment

Have trainees complete this sentence in their journals. "If I were training me to do my new job, I would . . .

Supervisors

Emphasize to new employees that asking supervisors questions is important when information isn't clear. Point out that knowing the evaluation process is important to one's job security.

> *Note: If you are training for a particular organization, explain the company's supervisor role in a new employee's training and evaluation.*

Co-workers

Point out that observing co-workers should be done wisely. Sometimes a supervisor will team a new worker with a co-worker as part of the training process. If, on the other hand, a new worker chooses the co-worker, it should be someone who is a reliable worker. Listening to the co-worker talk about the job, the supervisor, and other workers is helpful to a new worker; however, take caution if the information is overly critical.

Friends

Discuss why is it wise to talk to the supervisor before doing the work the way a friend has suggested.

Schools

Share any schools that offer adult and continuing education classes in your area.

Additional Activity: Research Continuing Education

Bring in catalogs from schools in your area offering courses in adult and continuing education. Divide into small groups. Give the group a list of various jobs such as receptionist, mechanic, nursing aide, retail salesperson, cook, etc. Have each group list the courses offered at different schools that would be helpful for each job.

> *Note:* If you are training for a particular organization, discuss any benefits the company offers to employees who update their skills through additional training. Does the company pay for classes? What are the grade point requirements? What are the requirements for reimbursement? Will additional training result in a pay raise or a promotion?

Additional Activity: Campus Visit

Visit a community college, vocational school, or a school offering continuing education classes. Give your trainees an opportunity to experience this type of atmosphere. Ask the school counselor to talk to the group about the classes available.

Additional Activity: Guest Speaker

Ask a continuing education or adult education advisor to speak about available opportunities to improve job skills. Discuss how the classes are conducted. How much hands-on experience is available?

Reading

Discuss the resources available on material about various occupations. Share any books or magazines you may have on this subject. Ask each individual to do the exercise at the end of the section.

Have the group share any resources they used that aren't a part of the list.

Additional Activity: Finding Job Descriptions

Divide the group into research groups of two or three members. Give them a list of various occupations and ask them to write a job description for each one. They will need to visit the library for this and document their sources.

To add interest to this project, do a little research, place some unusual occupations in each list.

Applying What You've Learned

Have the group read and do the case studies in this section. Discuss the case studies and the solutions to the problems.

Continuing the Learning Process

Not everyone learns at the same rate or in the same way. To learn at their maximum, each person needs to know their learning style. Although an individual may not always be able to use their preferred style, knowing this information enables them to learn more easily. It will also give them more confidence in their ability to learn. Seeing learning style as a part of our unique personality enables us to avoid comparing ourselves with other learners. It helps us accept ourselves.

Additional Activity: Business Changes

Make a list of the changes that might occur in a business requiring a worker to obtain additional learning.

Education for Life

Ask the group to read through this section. Fill in the checklist on learning styles and rank the three most frequently used methods. As a group go through the checklist and rank the most frequently used learning methods.

> *Note:* This group ranking could help you choose activities for the remainder of the course or workshop. Keeping a record of this information as you continue to teach the course may give you some ideas on improving the instruction. For example, if you have lots of people listing observing in the top three learning styles, you might decide to use more videos or demonstrations for group instruction. If only a few trainees list this method, you might consider reducing the use of this tech nique.

Steps to Learning

Have the group read this section. Go through the learning steps, discussing each one and what needs to be done to reach one's goal.

Additional Activity: Case Study

Use the following case study as a basis for understanding the steps to learning. After reading the case study, plan the learning steps Drew needs to take. Write them on a flip chart or overhead as a large group activity, or divide into small groups using a hand-out as a guide. Encourage the group to use their own imaginations as to the resources and reasons for Drew's answers. They will need to be "Drew" for this exercise.

Drew's Learning Project

Drew has worked at the Tippecanoe Valley Bank for two years. Recently, the bank manager told Drew that the bank has ordered personal computers for each of the employees in Drew's department. The computers will arrive in three months. The employees are expected to be proficient on the computers within six months.

Drew has had one community college computer course, in addition to a high school course. His friend, Kari, is a computer store salesperson. Drew is very excited about this modernization of his workplace and anxious to get started.

Step 1: What is Drew's motivation?

_____
_____
_____
_____
_____

Step 2: When he is done, what does Drew want to accomplish?

_____
_____
_____
_____
_____

Step 3: What are Drew's resources?

_____
_____
_____
_____
_____

Step 4: What are Drew's best resources?

_____
_____
_____
_____
_____

Step 5: When will Drew schedule this project?

_____
_____
_____
_____

Step 6: What questions does Drew need answered to learn this task?

Who? _____
What? _____
Why? _____
When? _____
How? _____

Step 7: What could Drew do to ensure he completes the project?

_____
_____
_____
_____
_____

Step 8: How could Drew practice what he has learned?

_____
_____
_____
_____
_____

Step 9: How can Drew evaluate progress on his learning project?

_____
_____
_____
_____
_____

Personal Learning Project

This exercise is designed to help trainees plan individual learning projects. Give trainees time to fill out the questionnaire and share learning projects. Encourage trainees to follow through on their plans when they are completed.

Applying What You've Learned

Divide into small groups. Have the group read and do the case studies. I recommend using the questions under "Personal Learning Project" as a guide in planning. Allow time for each group to complete their project. Then review the case studies together and record the group's responses. The format might be:

Skill Desired:_____

Person's Motivation: _____

Possible Resources: _____

Best Resources: _____

Time Schedule: _____

Progress Evaluation: _____

Practice Skill:_____

Summary

Read the chapter summary. Use the following questions to focus on the importance of continued learning.

- What types of learning can you use to learn new skills?
- Why is continued learning important to an employee?

Chapter Six

Knowing Yourself

Chapter Purpose

> *The purpose of this chapter is to make each trainee more aware of their own skills. Using a skills checklist, each trainee will discover hidden skills valued in the workplace. Throughout the chapter, the reader is encouraged to view themselves in a positive way. Despite what others may indicate, each of us is responsible for forming positive or negative feelings about ourselves.*

Blind, deaf, and unable to speak, the child's world was enclosed within the fenced yard of her home. Yet she grew to be a world traveler, a speaker, and a writer. Helen Keller became so well-known that a Broadway play told her success story.

Black, poor, and raised by a single parent, Dr. Ben Carson is recognized world-wide as a gifted neurosurgeon. He led the first surgical team to successfully separate Siamese twins joined at the head. Yet when he began practicing at John Hopkins University Medical Center, nurses and patients often mistook him for an orderly.

What makes some people succeed despite hindrances in their lives? What makes others fail despite talents they possess? In his book, *Gifted Hands*, Dr. Carson contends our inability to THINK BIG often prevents us from achieving our greatest successes in life.

No one can really "think big" unless they have a positive self-concept. In the workplace, employers are looking for people with confidence. Such employees are more motivated on the job. They are more creative in their work. These are traits employers want in their employees.

Your Self-Concept

Read the introduction. Discuss the terms self-concept, self-image, and self-esteem. Consider the reasons an employee with self-confidence would be more valuable to an employer.

Read the next two sections. Discuss the "outside influences" on one's self-concept. Remember that influences may be both positive and negative.

Additional Activity: **Personal Influences**

To illustrate the "outside" influences, ask each person to draw their personal circle of influence. Have them draw themselves in the middle of the circle. Then they should place around themselves the people (family, other workers, etc.), organizations (church, school, club), resources, (money, car, home), or activities (hobbies, athletics, etc.) that influence how they feel about themselves.

Discuss self-awareness. Some possible discussion questions are: What is self-awareness? Why is it important to know what skills you have? How will knowing yourself affect your self-concept?

Additional Activity: **This Is Me**

To help trainees get to know themselves, use this exercise. Ask each person to create a word picture of themselves. They are to make a list of nouns describing themselves. To get them started, demonstrate by describing yourself. Use the following format, substituting your name and descriptive nouns:

Verne is a:

- Trekie
- husband
- writer
- father
- book worm
- stamp collector
- junk food junkie
- football fan

After each individual has completed their list, divide into pairs and share discoveries. You may wish to exchange partners and continue sharing one or two more times.

> *Note: If you are working in a one-to-one situation, you may make a list yourself and share it with the trainee.*

Applying What You've Learned

Allow time for each individual to read and do the case studies. Discuss each case study and the questions.

> *Note: If you are working in a one-to-one situation, point out the reasons this trainee was hired for their position. Discuss the skills they possess that got them the job.*

Learn to Believe in Yourself

Read this section. List circumstances that might affect someone's self-concept in a negative way. (Divorce, a poor grade, loosing one's job, being rejected by a friend, being criticized, etc.) Consider the following questions: How could one's self-awareness be important when facing negative circumstances? What effect could one's self-awareness have on work relationships?

Additional Activity: Guest Speaker

Check with local resources like the local Mental Health Association for information available on forming a good self-concept. If they have a Speaker's Bureau, ask if they provide a speaker to talk to the group on ways to improve one's self-concept.

Exercise: Journal Assignment

Have students use the following fantasy to write a journal article. You have been granted a special wish. You may change anything about yourself that you wish. Write about what you will change. Write about what you will keep the same.

How You Look at Life

> *Note: Before starting this section, explain to the trainees that the "Your Approach to Life Quiz" is private. It is intended for their own use. Scores will not be revealed in class.*

Allow time for each individual to complete the quiz. Explain the scoring method. Allow time for scoring. Go through the scoring interpretation. Allow each person to interpret their own score.

You Can Teach Yourself to View Life Positively

Read this section. Point out that even if someone has a poor self-concept they can learn to believe in themselves. How can a person develop a positive attitude about life? Each person needs to take credit for their success. Failures too, should be analyzed to find their cause. Discuss the tips given by Joe Girard. How could these tips improve one's self-image?

©1993, JIST Works, Inc. • Indianapolis, Indiana

Personal Evaluation Exercise

> *Note: This may be difficult for some people to complete, especially someone lacking self-confidence. Encourage everyone to complete this exercise. Point out the need to look for everyday successes—not just monumental ones.*

Allow enough time for each individual to complete this exercise. Divide into pairs and share responses. (You may want to allow individuals to choose their own partners since some items might be more personal.)

Discuss the lessons of this exercise. Everyone has successes and failures in life. Success should be viewed as a time for reward. Failure should be viewed as a time to improve.

Your Job and Your Self-Concept

Read this section. Use the following questions for discussion.

Fact 1: You will make mistakes

- How should you react when you make a mistake?
- What is the best way to react to criticism from your supervisor?

Fact 2: Your employer wants you to succeed

- Why do you think your employer hired you?
- How should you react to compliments from your supervisor?

Additional Activity: Please Flatter Yourself

Divide into groups of two. Have each partner write a note complimenting the other person. (It may be written in letter form.) When finished, ask each writer to read their note to their partner. After each person has written and read their notes, discuss the feelings this exercise produced. Ask the students:

- Was it easier to write the compliment or read it?
- How did you feel when complimented?
- Was it easier to compliment or be complimented?
- What is the value of a compliment?

Identifying Your Skills

Use this section to emphasize your trainees' individual skills. Discovering these skills will add to each person's self-awareness. Encourage each trainee to think positively about themselves as they do this exercise. Point out that skills are divided into the three areas listed in *Job Savvy*.

Self-Management Skills

Discuss the meaning of self-management skills. These skills are basic to keeping a job. Many of these skills are reflected in the way a person approaches their personal life. Some of these skills are a part of one's personality. Others are skills that have to do with getting along with others and adapting to various job situations. Go through the list of skills in the checklist. Be sure the group understands the meaning of each skill. Why would an employer value this skill? Explain how to score the checklist. Give the group time to check and score the checklist.

Transferable Skills

Discuss the meaning of transferable skills. These are skills that are used in more than one job. These skills are important to getting promotions and raises. Go through the checklist. Be sure the group understands the meaning of each skill. Notice the skills are listed under various headings describing their usefulness in the workplace. Give time for the group to complete and score the checklist.

Job-Related Skills

Discuss the meaning of job-related skills. These skills have been developed through life experiences. Because they reflect personal interests, these skills are used in a job that is particularly attractive. Allow time for each trainee to fill in the job-related skills section. Point out the method used to score the job-related skills.

A Review of Your Skills

Read this section. Have the trainees record the scores from each of the skills areas. Ask trainees the questions below:

- Why is knowing your skills your strongest point as an employee?
- Did anyone discover a skill they weren't aware of having or aren't using?
- Did anyone find a weak skill? How could they improve this skill? Allow time for each student to write a short statement expressing their feelings after identifying their skills.

Additional Activity: Video Presentation

Show the video *Identifying Your Skills: A Job Search Essential*. This video shows many basic skills that are overlooked in a job interview. This video is available through JIST Works, Inc. and described in their catalog.

Applying What You've Learned

Divide into small groups. Discuss the case studies and answer the questions after each case study.

Summary

Discuss the five tips to help you believe in yourself. A healthier self-image takes time and work, but is possible with a positive outlook on life. Challenge each person to think of one success they have had during this *Job Savvy* experience. How will they reward themselves for their success?

- Think positive
- Accept compliments
- Accept responsibility
- Identify your skills
- Reward yourself

Chapter Seven

Getting Along with Your Supervisor

Chapter Purpose

> *The purpose of this chapter is to provide trainees with some facts about supervisors and their relationship with employees. Through the exercises and case studies in this chapter, the trainee has the opportunity to view the workplace from a supervisor's perspective.*

©1993, JIST Works, Inc. • Indianapolis, Indiana

Dagwood has Mr. Dithers. Fred Flintstone has Mr. Slade. Lois Lane has Perry White. On or off the job, everyone has a boss, but not everyone wants to admit it. In today's society, many young people grow up without an authority figure to serve as a role model. This means that many young employees are entering the work force not knowing "Who's the boss?" Often this leads to problems which result in dismissal. Many entry-level employees have no idea what responsibilities their supervisor has. They may, in fact, view the supervisor's job as easy. From their point of view, the supervisor stands back and bosses while the other employees do the dirty work. The supervisor may even be viewed as the "enemy" constantly looking over each worker's shoulder watching for mistakes.

Understanding the importance of good relationships with supervisors is vital to trainees. They need to know that supervisors play an important role in their success and happiness on the job. The supervisor often has great influence in such matters as promotions, salary increases, and employee dismissal.

> *Note: A perspective employer will be impressed by a good recommendation from one's supervisor.*

Work Team Concept

Many businesses function as work teams with supervisors acting as team leaders. This introduces the idea of a co-operative venture between a supervisor and each team worker. Supervisors and workers depend on each other.

After completing this chapter, the trainees will have the answers to the following questions:

- What do supervisors do?
- What do supervisors expect from workers?
- How does a supervisor judge an employee's work?
- Why is it important for employees to maintain a healthy relationship with their supervisors?
- What if a supervisor and an employee disagree?

Supervising Is a Job

Read the chapter introduction. Discuss the definition of supervision. Point out that co-operation between supervisors and workers is very important to the success of any business.

Additional Activity: Create a Supervisor

Divide into groups of two to three members. Provide each group with a large sheet of newsprint and markers or crayons. Ask each group to draw a supervisor and the equipment needed to do their job. Provide a large group setting to share these creations.

Additional Activity: Supervisor Definition

Divide into groups of three or four members. Ask each group to define the word "supervision". List the responsibilities of a supervisor. Share this information in a large group setting.

Additional Activity: Egg-jective

Review the definitions of supervision. Consider a supervisor's objective in order to get the "what we want" from each of the following businesses. Using an egg to represent the "what we have," what would the supervisor encourage workers to do to get the end product?

This may be a large group activity using as many of the suggested businesses as you wish. You may want to divide into groups of three to four members, assigning different businesses to each group. In this case, have each group make a list of what the supervisor would do to get the end result. The following chart may be used on a flip chart or as a handout for small groups.

BUSINESS	WHAT WE HAVE	WHAT WE WANT	WHAT WORKERS MUST DO
Grocery Store			
Bakery			
Restaurant			
Chicken Farm			
Zoo			
Alligator Farm			
Fish Hatchery			
Pet Shop			

©1993, JIST Works, Inc. • Indianapolis, Indiana

Your Supervisor Is the Team Leader in the Business World

Read this section of *Job Savvy*. Look at the various titles given a supervisor—leader, coach, cheerleader, teacher, and counselor. Discuss these titles as related to a supervisor's work.

Read the box entitled "Delegate." Discuss the meaning of the word delegate. Ask trainees the following questions:

- Why is delegating necessary?
- What problems might result when a supervisor delegates work?
- What problems might result if a supervisor doesn't delegate work?
- Who is responsible for the problems that may result in each situation?

> *Note:* Point out that when a supervisor delegates a job to an employee, trust is placed in the employee and their ability to complete the task.

Additional Activity: Trust Walk

This activity will illustrate the feelings and trust involved in delegating tasks. Ask each person to find a partner. One will be the leader; the other the follower.

> *Note:* No one should be forced to participate in this activity. Give an opportunity to "sit this one out" if anyone is reluctant to take part.

No talking is allowed during the trust walk. On signal from the instructor, the follower, with eyes closed, is guided through the designated area by the leader. The leader should do this in an interesting, but safe way. This activity should take place for at least five minutes. If the designated area is outside, it could take place for a longer time. Stop the walk and talk about the feelings each group experienced. Ask the following questions:

- How did the followers feel?
- Did anyone open their eyes during the walk? Why?
- How did the leaders feel?
- Was there a temptation to talk to the follower rather than just to guide? Why?

Apply these feelings to a supervisor trusting a new employee to do a task.

What Does a Supervisor Do?

Assign this section for individual completion. Allow time to complete this work. Divide into small groups and ask each group to compare their ratings and the reasons for these ratings. Ask each group to make a list of responsibilities they believe the supervisor couldn't delegate. As a large group, make a list of the responsibilities that the supervisor couldn't delegate. Discuss the following:

- Why would these jobs not be delegated?
- Are there any jobs that the supervisor would never do?

It's Not as Easy as It Looks

Read this section together. Discuss the following question: "How can an employee understand a supervisor's responsibilities in the workplace?"

Communicating with Your Supervisor

Briefly point out the five essentials for good communication with one's supervisor as listed.

Rely on Your Senses When Following Instructions

Read this section of *Job Savvy*. With the trainees, go through the list step by step. Discuss the problems that might be encountered as instructions are given in an on-the-job situation. Concentration is important—especially if machinery is making listening difficult. In such situations, asking the supervisor to repeat instructions may be necessary.

Emphasize that asking questions is important, but that a supervisor should be given the opportunity to give the information before questions are asked. Repeatedly asking the same question might annoy a supervisor. Suggest writing the answer down if trainees have trouble remembering.

> *Note:* If you are training for a particular organization, use this time to demonstrate any task that a new trainee may need to learn.

Additional Activity: Nonverbal Communication

Discuss what is meant by nonverbal communication such as body language and gestures or voice inflections. Make a list of these types of communication. What can they indicate to an employee? Some suggestions might be: pointing to an object, raising an eyebrow, whispering, frowning, waving one's hands, stepping back from a person, raising one's voice, and placing one's hands on one's hips.

Additional Activity: Video Presentation

View a 10-15 minute teaching or demonstration video on any subject. Turn off the audio. As trainees watch the video, ask them to make a list of all the non-verbal communication they observe. Discuss the nonverbal communication and indications.

> *Note: If it is helpful to the group's understanding, view the video a second time using the audio.*

Additional Activity: Follow Directions

Ask a resource person to visit the classroom to demonstrate a local craft. After the demonstration, allow the group to make the craft following the demonstrator's directions.

> *Jargon: Read the box "Jargon." Although learning this new "language" may be difficult, it is a part of the job. Emphasize that trainees should ask questions if they don't understand what is meant by a particular term.*

Additional Activity: Word Game

To illustrate the different uses of words, write the phrase "a vehicle with four wheels" on the flip chart or overhead. Ask the group to brainstorm as many other words that could suggest a vehicle with four wheels as they can think of. List the words. Point out how each word meets the definition, but has a different meaning.

> *Note: If you are training for a particular organization, explain any jargon that is commonly used in that business.*

Understanding Instructions

Have the group close their books. Give each person a blank sheet of paper 8 1/2 inches by 11 inches. Read the four-step directions under "Understanding Instructions" one step at a time, however, don't repeat the directions.

Now have the group open their books. Instruct them to read and do the exercise under "Understanding Instructions." Allow time to discuss their answers at the end of this exercise.

Asking Questions

Read this section. Discuss the three points about asking questions. Ask the following questions:

- Why is asking right away important?
- What if the supervisor isn't available to ask?
- How does summarizing responses help workers?
- How does summarizing responses help supervisors?
- Why is memorization important?
- If you have problems memorizing, how can you keep from repeating questions?

©1993, JIST Works, Inc. • Indianapolis, Indiana

Additional Activity: **Learning to Ask Questions**

The following case studies will help trainees know how to phrase questions for their supervisors. In each case a problem has occurred in the workplace and the supervisor is presenting the problem to the employee or employees. Using the old newspaper questions (who? what? where? when? why? and how?), have the trainees find the information given by the supervisor. If information isn't given to answer one of the questions, have the group form a question that would give the information they need. I have devised the following worksheet for use in completing the exercise.

Learning to Ask Questions Worksheet

Case Study #1

Nelson is the head waiter at "The Eatery." He is holding a meeting of all the serving personnel before the evening shift begins.

"Last night several customers complained that the back dining room wasn't being served quickly. Complaints ranged from cold food to lack of refills on coffee. There was a team of three on duty back there, but since that area has been designated as the non-smoking section, more diners are asking to eat in that area. So, I'm putting two more people on the crew for this evening's dinner hour. Let's go now, it's time to get on the floor."

What is the problem?
_____
_____
_____

Where did the problem occur?
_____
_____
_____

Who will be involved in solving the problem?
_____
_____
_____

How will the problem be solved?
_____
_____
_____

What question would you ask if Nelson was your supervisor?
_____
_____
_____

©1993, JIST Works, Inc. • Indianapolis, Indiana

Case Study #2

Mary is the head nurse in the hospital maternity ward. One of the new mothers has developed an infection. Mary is holding a briefing at shift change.

"Mrs. Johnson has a staph infection and she can't remain in the maternity area of the hospital. Josh and Suzanne, I'll need your help."

What is the problem?
_____
_____
_____

When did the problem occur?
_____
_____
_____

Where did the problem occur?
_____
_____
_____

Who will be involved in solving the problem?
_____
_____
_____

How will the problem be solved?
_____
_____
_____

What question would you ask if Mary was your supervisor?
_____
_____
_____

Case Study #3

Jolene is a toy store manager. She is having a sales meeting with the store employees.

"Squirt gun sales are below normal for August. We are over stocked and have to get rid of them before the end of the month."

What is the problem?
___
___
___

When did the problem occur?
___
___
___

Where did the problem occur?
___
___
___

Who will be involved in solving the problem?
___
___
___

How will the problem be solved?
___
___
___

What question would you ask if Jolene was your supervisor?
___
___
___

Reporting the Results

Read this section and discuss each point. Emphasize the need for the employee to take the responsibility of developing communication between themselves and the supervisor.

Additional Activity: Role Play

Divide into groups of three members to role play the situations below. Each group should have one person playing the role of the supervisor, one person the employee, and the third person is the observer. The observer should point out any clear or unclear communication that occurs between the supervisor and the employee.

> *Note:* Give each group a copy of these situations to role play. Have the members of the group change roles after each situation is completed.

Situation #1

The supervisor asks the employee to restock the toppings in the ice cream bar. The employee has completed the job.

Situation #2

The supervisor told the employee to make 15 copies of a memo. The memo is addressed to all employees. The employee knows that there are 25 people in the office.

Situation #3

The supervisor places the employee in the appliance section of the store. The employee has never worked in appliances. A customer wants to know which refrigerator is more energy efficient.

Taking Messages

Read this section and point out the necessary steps to accurately record the message.

Additional Activity: Telephone Conversation Role Play

One trainee poses as the caller. Use another trainee as the message taker. Have the rest of the group record the information given on a message pad. The information should be heard, not read by the message taker. This makes it more like a telephone conversation.

Call #1

Samantha Trumpet is calling for Louis Tamborine, the manager of the Pied Piper Music Store. She wants a donation for an upcoming carnival at a local school. Her number is 752-5001.

Call #2

Don Iron is calling for Pamela Wholesome, the head dietitian at the Cedar Creek Care Center. He is unable to get individual cups of chocolate swirl ice cream and wants to know if another flavor would be acceptable. His business phone is 476-3300 extension 35.

Call #3

Dr. Brace's office is calling for Stan Outback. His Friday after noon appointment has been cancelled because the doctor is leaving town. Call 391-4065 to reschedule.

Communicating About Job Performance

Read this section. Discuss the importance of listening to the supervisor about one's job performance. Point out that some of this communication will be informal. This could include words of encouragement while working, or demonstrating an easier way to get the job done. Some of this job performance communication will be more formal. This could include private discussions or reviewing a performance evaluation form. Whatever the type of communication, these are good points for trainees to remember:

- **Don't respond to feedback with anger:** Sometimes feedback from a supervisor may be negative. Discuss the best way to handle negative feedback. Suggest ways to handle one's emotions in such situations. Discuss appropriate trainee responses if supervisors shout.

- **Know what it is you have done wrong:** Remind trainees to ask questions. If the supervisor is angry, the employee should calmly apologize and ask how to do a correct job the next time.

- **Thank supervisors for compliments:** Point out that a simple "thank you" from the trainee lets the supervisor know their attention is appreciated. No one enjoys being ignored when they give a compliment.

- **Ask for feedback:** What if a supervisor is a "clam?" Point out that asking for feedback about work habits is a good idea. It shows job interest. It also tells a supervisor their opinion is valued.

Additional Activity: Criticism Evaluation Self-Test

This exercise allows trainees to recognize their personal reactions to criticism.

Mark the items listed on the next page with "yes" or "no." Be honest. This quiz will give you an idea of your attitude about accepting criticism. It will help you see ways you can improve your attitude and behavior when you are criticized.

CRITICISM EVALUATION SELF TEST

QUESTION	YES	NO
Do you avoid your supervisor when you make mistakes?		
Do you get angry when your supervisor criticizes you?		
Do you use other employees' poor work as an excuse for yours?		
Do you give excuses for your mistakes?		
Do you avoid admitting that you made a mistake?		
Do you feel personally attacked when you are criticized by your supervisor?		
Do you need to defend yourself when you are criticized?		
Do you need to talk back to your supervisor?		
Do you need to prove you are right and your supervisor is wrong?		
Do you pout after you have been criticized?		
Do you talk to co-workers about your supervisor's criticism?		
Do you always believe your supervisor's criticism is unfair		
Do you criticize your supervisor after he/she criticizes you?		
Do you continue to think about the criticism afterward for a long period of time?		
Do you shout back at your supervisor if he/she shouts?		
Do you criticize your supervisor behind his/her back?		
Do you think about quitting when you are criticized?		
Do you ignore your supervisor's criticism?		

Note: You may want the group to divide into small groups to discuss the quiz items. In this case, give the scoring information after the small group discussion.

©1993, JIST Works, Inc. • Indianapolis, Indiana

Scoring the Criticism Evaluation Self-Test

This quiz was made to get trainees thinking about criticism. No one can do everything the right way every time. At some time in our work experience, we will receive criticism. This quiz shows the areas that may need improvement in order to use criticism in a positive way.

The quiz was designed with "no" being the preferred answer. Award 5 points for each "yes." Use the following table to evaluate your use of criticism.

- 20 Points or Below—You accept criticism very well.
- 20-30 Points—You accept criticism in a satisfactory way.
- 30-40 Points—You accept criticism in a fairly good way.
- Above 40 Points—You need to work on this skill.

> *Performance Appraisal:* Read the box "Performance Appraisal." Discuss what might happen in a performance appraisal session with a supervisor. If you can obtain some samples of forms used in evaluations, share them with the group.

> *Note:* If you are training for a particular organization, discuss the evaluation process used for new employees in that company.

Applying What You've Learned

Allow time for individuals to record their answers for each case study. Discuss the case studies and the answers with the group.

Meeting a Supervisor's Expectations

Read and discuss the introduction to this section. Emphasize the fact that a supervisor is involved with many workers. Their problems are multiplied when several workers break "little" rules.

> *Note:* Don't assume that the trainees know how to practice these six behaviors. Although these six items are basic knowledge, many new workers have lost jobs because they didn't practice one of them. Take the time to read and discuss each point.

List each of the six behaviors as the group discusses each one. Make sure the group understands what each point means and how it should be practiced. Emphasize their importance. Be specific as to the meaning of each behavior. Use the information and questions in *Job Savvy* as a guide for the discussion. The trainees should fill in the information under each behavior as it is discussed.

Applying What You've Learned

Divide into small groups. Using the case studies, ask each group to find the "mosquito" and the result in each case. Review each group's conclusions.

Resolving Problems with Your Supervisor

Problems do occur between supervisors and employees. People don't always agree. The trainees need to know how to communicate respectfully with their supervisor when disagreements occur. In this section, three methods are given for resolving conflicts.

Introduce this section by reading this paragraph. Briefly give a definition of each procedure. Write them on a flip chart or overhead.

Conflict resolution means talking to your supervisor about the disagreement. You or your supervisor may initiate this.

Grievance procedure is filing a formal complaint about the disagreement. Some forms will probably be involved. Other people such as a personal director or a chief executive officer may be involved. In some cases, a union representative would guide the employee throughout the process. The employee initiates this procedure.

Disciplinary action means your supervisor is unhappy with your job performance. This is a formal procedure set up by the company. It varies from company to company. Your supervisor initiates this procedure.

Conflict Resolution

Allow time for the group to read this section. Go through the six suggestions given to help solve conflicts. Discuss each point.

Additional Activity: Language Resolution

Using the six guidelines listed under "Conflict Resolution" in *Job Savvy*, restate the following negative statements in a way that will help solve the conflict rather than cause more problems. Each statement is made by an **employee** to a **supervisor**.

> *Note: If this is used as a large group activity, the negative statements could be written on a flip chart or overhead. The group would make the positive statements orally.*

This could also be used as an individual or small group activity. The negative statements would be written on the worksheet, allowing a blank area for rewriting each statement.

Conflict Resolution Worksheet

1. You never told me to fill the ice tubs. How was I supposed to know?

2. If I can't have this weekend off, I'm quitting.

3. Sometime when you have a chance could you and I talk about this problem I'm having?

4. You give me less hours than any of the other people who work here.

5. You ordered too many copies of this book and now you expect me to sell them. Forget it! It's your mistake.

6. You should have told me sooner. Thursday night is my bowling league. I can't work late.

7. So I jammed up the copier. It's not like you never made a mistake.

8. I know what I know. Mary Alice told Troy, who told me just what you said about my not getting that promotion.

9. Well, you can't fool me. I heard there's going to be a big lay-off next month.

10. You are always in the back room when the evening rush starts.

Grievance Procedures

Allow time for the group to read this section. Discuss the seriousness and complications of the grievance procedures. Note that such a step will cause stress between an employee and a supervisor. Point out that in some cases this is a necessary step; however, it should always be done with much thought first.

Additional Activity: **Guest Speaker**

Invite a union representative to explain their part in dealing with the grievance procedure.

> *Note: If you are training for a particular organization, explain the grievance procedure used by that company.*

Disciplinary Action

Allow time for the group to read this section. Discuss the four disciplinary steps and explain each step.

Note that an oral warning is the first step. If taken seriously, an employee should be able to correct the problem without any further discipline. Employers seldom want to fire someone unless it is absolutely necessary.

At times an employee should look for another job. When might it be wise for an employee to look for another job?

> *Note: If you are training for a particular organization, be sure to discuss the disciplinary policy of that business.*

Summary

Read the summary at the end of the chapter. Important discussion questions to ask are:

- Why is it important for an employee to maintain a healthy relationship with their supervisor?
- What if a supervisor and an employee disagree?

Chapter Eight
Getting Along with Other Workers

Chapter Purpose

The purpose of this chapter is to show trainees the reasons and methods to be an effective team player. Since individuals are unique, the need for tolerance in the workplace is obvious. The trainee is given opportunities to find solutions to problems that might develop between co-workers. Knowing how to approach special problems will prepare them for the real work world.

©1993, JIST Works, Inc. • Indianapolis, Indiana

One of my greatest summer pleasures was watching my sons' T-ball games. (T-ball is an introduction to the game of baseball.) Players are assigned various field positions; however, the pitcher doesn't pitch. Batters hit the ball while it is setting on a rubber post called the tee. No one sits on the bench in a T-ball game. Everybody plays. Since there are often between 15 and 20 children on a team, the outfield has lots of coverage. Occasionally a real slugger enters the batter's box. With one fierce swing, they send the ball into the outfield. The outfielders go wild as each child tries desperately to grab the ball from the other. That's when you suddenly realize your child isn't a team player.

Teamwork is important. On the playing field, a sports team that can't work together will often be unsuccessful. In the laboratory, a team of scientists will achieve more discoveries as they share ideas. Even at home, sharing household duties will get the job done quicker and allow leisure time for everyone.

In the workplace, teamwork has become increasingly more common. Managers and supervisors have been trained to organize workers into teams. They view themselves as team leaders. They expect each person to co-operate in achieving the same goal. It is vital that trainees understand the importance of getting along with other workers.

Team Concept

Introduce this chapter by discussing the following questions:

- What is a team?
- Why are teams used in the workplace?
- How does the teamwork approach affect a supervisor's perception of his workers?
- How does the teamwork approach affect the relationships between co-workers?

Additional Activity: Tinker Toys

To introduce the idea of teamwork, divide the group into work teams of four people. Place a Tinker Toy sculpture on a table for group observation. Allow observation for 1 minute before covering the sculpture.

Give each group a set of just enough Tinker Toys necessary to create the same sculpture. Their job is to recreate the sculpture using all the pieces. Emphasize that this is a **team** effort. Allow each group time to complete their sculptures. Uncover the original sculpture for comparison.

> *Note:* Privately ask one member of each team to observe the other team members as they complete this task.

Using the following questions, the observers should record their impressions of how the group handled this problem.

- Was there a group leader? Who?
- How did the group react to the leader?
- If there was no leader, how did the group organize to solve the problem?
- Was there disagreement in the group? How was this approached?
- Would assigning a leader help the team work any more efficiently?

Discuss the information each observer has collected.

Get to Know Your Co-workers

Ask the group to read the introduction to this exercise. Have each individual do the exercise following the instructions in *Job Savvy*. Then go through the list together, discussing why each person chose "yes" or "no."

There may be some disagreement since not everyone will view the situations in quite the same way.

How You Fit In

Read this section together and use the questions for group discussion.

Know your position

- Why is it important to know what other workers expect?
- Can anyone in the group relate a work situation that involves team members doing a task in a particular way?
- Why might a new worker be expected to do the "dirty work" such as cleaning up at the end of the day?
- Why should a new worker do this type of task?

Accept good-natured teasing

- Why do co-workers tease and play jokes on new workers?
- What is the best reaction to such joking?
- If the teasing becomes a problem, why would it be wise to talk to the co-worker first rather than going to the supervisor?
- What is the difference between joking and harassment?

> *Note: Harassment and discrimination will be discussed further later in this chapter.*

Do your fair share
- Name a situation where someone didn't do their part of a task. How did you react to the situation? How did you feel about that person?
- Name a situation where someone did the whole task rather than let others help. How did you react to the situation? How did you feel toward that person?
- When is it wisest to do what the supervisor says?

Don't do other people's work
- Why is it unwise to do other people's work?
- Is it ever wise to help someone else with their work?
- What should you do if you have completed all of your work and there is still time in the work day?
- If you have completed all of your work, is it alright to do someone else's work?

Know how your team functions within the organization
- Why is it important to understand how other teams effect your work?
- Who is responsible for problems that develop between teams within the organization?

> *Note: Emphasize that becoming a part of the team takes time. Point out that both the established team and the new worker are adjusting to the situation. If new workers remain calm and accept their position as the newcomer, this process will go more smoothly.*

Additional Activity: Synergy

To introuce the phenomenon of synergy, divide the participants in half. Explain that each group will be manufacturing paper chains. You will need to supply glue and pre-cut paper strips (1/2" x 4-1/4 ") for each participant.

Instruct the first group to form teams of three. Give the teams time to plan how they will perform this task.

While they are planning, explain to the second group that they will work alone. They are not to communicate with each other in any way.

Allow the two groups to begin working at the same time. After 5-10 minutes, stop the workers. Compare the work of the two groups. The teams of three should have produced the longer chains.

Applying What You've Learned

Allow time for the group to do this exercise. Discuss the two case studies.

The Value of Difference

Read the introduction to this section.

Additional Activity: Character Study

This exercise is meant to help the group understand that individual differences make each person unique.

Divide the group into two teams. Have each person list five characteristics that make them unique. This may include something they can do, a personality trait, a hereditary characteristic, etc. Have them sign the paper. Collect papers from each team keeping the two teams' papers separated.

Pick a paper and read the characteristics to the opposite team. This team has three guesses to identify the person. Score three points if they are correct on the first guess, two on the second guess, and 1 on the third guess. Continue play in the same manner with the opposing team.

When you have read all the papers, total the teams' scores. (You may hand out a small prize to the winning team.)

Additional Activity: Let Me Count the Ways

Brainstorm a list of all the ways that people in any given work situation may differ.

Values

Discuss what is meant by personal values. Give some examples of personal values. Discuss how these values are formed. Give an example of how people with differing values might strengthen a work team. Read and discuss each of the three general personality categories and the values associated with each. Have the group read and follow the instruction in the values exercise in *Job Savvy*.

Additional Activity: Categories

This activity could be used for discussion in a large or small group situation. It could also be used as a handout exercise for individuals.

Using the three general categories (traditionalist, humanist, and pragmatist) decide which type of person might have made each of these statements. Place a T (traditionalist), H (humanist), or P (pragmatist) in front of each statement.

____ I'm not working this weekend. I deserve a rest.

____ I'm expecting a promotion to assistant manager by next June.

____ This is the way my boss taught me to do it so that's how I do it.

____ I'm working next Saturday because the boss asked me to.

____ My boss called me in today. He congratulated me on getting the Thompson account finalized. I hope he is thinking of a raise.

____ I'm asking for next Saturday off. I have a hot date with Stan.

____ The manager was out of town today. I practically ran the office myself.

____ I'm signing up for the account course the company is offering next month

____ My company is opening a child care center for their workers. That's really progressive for them.

____ I plan to stay with my company till I retire.

Additional Activity: Value Comparison

Divide into groups of three or four members. Have each group list the values they have concerning the following issues that could be a part of their work situations. Have the groups compare values. Encourage each group to discuss what they believe influenced their values. Topics could include: paid vacations, company family outings, company-paid education, working overtime, changing jobs, getting a promotion, and merit pay raises

Effective Work Teams Blend Values

Read these two paragraphs. Discuss the need to have all types of people in a work team.

Find out how many people fit in each personality/value category. Ask each group to share their reasons for deciding which category they fall into. Point out that no value system is totally good or bad.

Temperaments

Read this section. What is temperament? Discuss each of the temperament types. Have the group read and follow the directions in the temperament exercise in *Job Savvy*.

Additional Activity: **Tempermental Journey**

Consider each of the temperament types. What type temperament might choose each of these occupations?

- Inventor
- Judge
- Scientist
- Soldier
- Cartoonist
- Teacher
- Police Officer
- Radio Disc Jockey
- Baseball Player
- Artist

How to Deal with Differences

Read the information in this section together. Discuss how to approach conflicting temperaments.

Additional Activity: **Temperaments Unite**

Ask the group to divide themselves into temperament groups. Give each of the groups the following problem. Have each group tell how the temperament group they represent would react to the problem. What would their solution be? Compare each group's reactions and solutions. Would the different reactions and solutions cause conflicts?

Jody, one of the people in your workplace, is causing problems. Although Jody has never attacked anyone physically, if there is a disagreement with other workers, Jody's behavior is often very aggressive. Your supervisor has talked to Jody, but the bullying still continues. Last week a new worker was so frightened that he resigned. Jody works at an acceptable pace and your supervisor indicates that Jody won't be let go. The work grapevine says that Jody is having problems at home also.

- How did your temperament group react to this problem?
- How did your temperament group solve this problem?
- How could differing temperaments affect the solution to this problem?

Individual Diversity

Have the class read this section. Ask the questions under each heading below to stimulate discussion.

Gender. Read this statement from *Job Savvy*:

"Women are usually more attentive to the needs of other people while men tend to be more aggressive and ambitious."

- How would this diversity strengthen a team in each of the following workplaces?
  - A used car dealership
  - A walk-in medical clinic
  - A computer store

©1993, JIST Works, Inc. • Indianapolis, Indiana

Ethnicity—Read this statement from *Job Savvy*

"Oriental cultures traditionally value cooperation, while western cultures emphasize individualism."

- How would this diversity strengthen a team in each of the following workplaces?
  - A hair salon
  - An elegant supper club
  - An auto repair shop

Age—Read this statement from *Job Savvy*

"Younger workers usually bring enthusiasm and energy into a job. Older workers bring patience and their experience."

- How would this diversity strengthen a team in each of the following workplaces? A hardware store, a floral shop, a bakery?

> *Note:* The possibility of young entry-level employees coming into contact with older retirees at the same job level is very real. With some people retiring as early as age 55, the potential of several additional years of employment still exists.

Early retirees sometimes choose a second career to supplement their retirement income, or to give them an opportunity to try something different. For some, the workplace is a way of having contact with other people after the loss of their lifetime partner. Whatever the reason, more and more older workers are entering the work force for the second time. Many businesses are hiring senior citizens on a part- or full-time basis. Often these positions are at entry level.

Exercise: Journal Assignment

Write a journal article using this topic: "I have a biased view about working with:

_____

_____

- I formed this bias because of:

_____

_____

_____

- I could overcome this bias by:

_____

_____

_____

> *Note:* Working with a physically or mentally handicapped person is another diversity that workers might encounter. For many, the adjustment to being near a handicapped person can be very awkward. Unfortunately most of us have formed biased views about handicapped people. We see the handicap rather than the individual. Because we focus on the handicap, we place ourselves in a more awkward situation.

Additional Activity: Is a Handicap Always Visible?

To help trainees become aware of various types of handicaps, brainstorm a list. Remember to include "unseen" handicaps such as diabetes, dyslexia, mental retardation, epilepsy, etc. Encourage anyone, who has had an experience with a handicapped person, to share with the group.

> *Note:* If there is a person with a handicap in your group, encourage that person to share his or her views and experiences.

Additional Activity: Attitude Check

Use the following quiz to help your students examine their attitudes toward handicapped people. Although the class shouldn't be required to reveal their answers, you may wish to discuss each statement examining the reason people might have the attitude.

Check Your Attitudes

Using the following statements, check your attitudes about handicapped people. Answer each statement with a true or false answer. Be honest.

___ Handicapped people feel sorry for themselves.

___ Mentally retarded people are always happy.

___ Blind people can't hear well

___ Handicapped people expect special treatment in the workplace.

___ A handicapped person can't be a contributing member of a work team.

___ Mentally retarded people are sexually over-stimulated.

___ Epilepsy is contagious.

___ The handicapped need someone else to handle their financial decisions.

___ The mentally retarded can't live independently.

___ Deaf people can't communciate intelligently with hearing people.

©1993, JIST Works, Inc. • Indianapolis, Indiana

Scoring Your Attitude Check

The right answer in this quiz is always "false." Have the students score 1 point for each correct answer. Using the following scoring system, have the students rate their attitude toward handicapped individuals.

- 10 Points—Excellent attitude
- 8-9 Points—Good attitude
- 7-6 Points—Poor attitude
- 5-0 Points—Need to improve attitude

Encourage your students to get to know handicapped individuals to broaden their perceptions. Handicapped people are individuals and should be treated as such.

Additional Activity: Guest Speaker

Check with the local speaker's bureau for any group or individual, who could share information about handicaps with the group. Sources for information on the handicapped include the local mental health association, the education department of a local hospital, or social service agencies in the area.

Some handicapped individuals are willing to share their experience with a group. This would give your class a terrific opportunity to realize that though handicaps happen to real people, the handicap isn't the person.

Another excellent source of information are local businesses. Ask a representative of a business that hires handicapped employees to relate their experiences.

Basic Human Relations

Read this section and discuss the 14 steps with the group.

Additional Activity: Can You Relate?

Divide into small groups of three or four members. Give each group a copy of the following exercise.

> *Note:* The group should read this section in the book before doing the exercise.

Basic Human Relations Worksheet

Using the 14 steps listed in this section, write the step number that offers the best reaction to each situation.

___ You have just walked into the break room. You overhear Pam and Rich talking about Nick's latest romantic antics.

___ Jane has asked you to join the company volleyball team.

___ You are upset because Ryan has been taking writing materials from your desk rather than getting his own supplies from the storage room.

___ Your supervisor says you need to speed up and get more work completed during the day. You have tried, but you aren't sure how to go about it.

___ At 9:30 Marcia asks you if you are ready for a break. Pable and Sy are going for a cup of coffee.

___ Last week when you were sick and missed a day of work, Jon typed up your report that was due that day.

___ Lonnie believes tha Nanette isn't doing her share of the work. He wants you to talk to the manager about it.

___ You like your new job, but you really miss your old friends at your former job.

___ Yesterday Luke put the wrong ingredients on a customer's pizza. He had to make a new pizza. The customer was really upset for having to wait so long for the order.

___ All the servers in the ice cream shop have to put together their own ice cream orders. At your former job, one person put together the sundaes and other ice cream orders. You think this system worked a lot smoother.

Applying What You've Learned

Discuss the ways that one can react positively and negatively. Emphasize that a positive approach offers reassurance and support to fellow workers. A negative approach can create uneasiness and even ill feelings between co-workers.

Using the case studies, divide into small groups. Have groups discuss each case study answering the questions listed in the book. Have each group share their conclusions as the class discusses each case study.

©1993, JIST Works, Inc. • Indianapolis, Indiana

Special Problems with Co-workers

Read the following sections together and discuss the issues and how they effect the workplace. The questions listed under each heading below are designed to increase awareness about these sensitive issues.

> *Note:* You, as the instructor, need to consider your group and which of the questions you will use, if any.

Sexual Harassment

- What types of conduct or behavior can be interpreted as sexual harassment?
- Could both a man or a woman be guilty of sexual harassment?
- Does sexual harassment involve only members of the opposite sex?
- Could the way one dresses be interpreted as a type of sexual harassment?
- Could certain speech phrases be interpreted as a type of sexual harassment?
- Why might an employer consider firing you if they believe you are guilty of sexual harassment?
- Sexual harassment charges don't always surface at the time of the incident. Why does this often happen? What effect does this have on the parties involved?
- Discuss what should be done if you are the victim of sexual harassment.

> *Note:* Point out that this is a very serious accusation that could affect a person's employment and reputation.

Racial Harassment

- What types of behavior could be interpreted as racial harassment?
- Is racial harassment usually the result of ignorance?
- If you are the victim of racial ignorance, how can you overcome your attitude?
- One of your co-workers is telling racial jokes. How would you handle this situation?
- One of your co-workers constantly uses an offensive racial slur when referring to another worker. How would you handle the situation?
- Discuss what you should do if you are the victim of racial harassment.

> *Note:* Again, point out the need to take such an accusation very seriously because of the damage it can cause.

Dating

- Why is dating a co-worker a real possibility for many people?
- When could dating a co-worker become sexual harassment?
- Why do some companies have a "no dating" policy? Does your company have such a policy?
- How can dating a co-worker cause problems in the workplace?
- You are dating a co-worker. What can you do to avoid situations that will cause conflict?

Summary

Read the chapter summary and answer the questions below.
- Why is teamwork so important in the workplace?
- In what ways are people different?
- How can differences make a work team stronger?

Chapter Nine

Problem-Solving Skills

Chapter Purpose

> *This chapter highlights the reasons employers are looking for workers with problem-solving skills. The trainees are introduced to a variety of ways to approach problems. They are encouraged to practice these problem-solving skills using their own creativity.*

Real simple! Right? Climb out of the car. Lock the door. Hurry into the restaurant. The waiter directs me to the correct dining room. No problem! I've arrived just in time for the staff luncheon. But wait a minute! Where are my car keys? Could it be?

Life is complicated and full of problems. Just when you least expect it those problem-solving skills are needed again.

The workplace is no exception to this rule. As organizations become more complicated, there is a greater need for workers to be able to solve problems. Workers with problem-solving capabilities will be highly valued by employers. Trainees need to understand that problem solving is a highly marketable skill.

Problem-Solving Skills Are Important

Emphasize that this chapter will help trainees become better problem solvers. Read the introduction to this chapter. It contains two problems. Ask your trainees to spot them.

Management Through Team Work and Employee Involvement

Ask the group to read this section, and the box on "Quality Circles." Discuss this material using the questions below as a guide.

- What is meant by employee involvement?
- Why are employees becoming more involved in problem solving?
- What is a quality circle?
- As an employee, would your attitude about your job change if you were a part of a quality circle? How?

Additional Activity: **Video Presentation**

Use one of the following 20 minute videos available through JIST Works, Inc., the publisher of this book.

- *Everyone a Problem Solver:* Presents the message that problem solving is highly prized in the workplace. Many of the examples in the video are in an office setting.
- *How to Succeed in the Changing Workplace:* Deals with changes that are taking place in business. These changes are affecting employees. This video illustrates the employees' need for problem-solving skills, especially in dealing with customers.

Problem Solving

Read "Basic Problem-Solving Assumptions." Discuss the three basic assumptions.

- Why is it important to believe that a problem can be solved?
- In what way is problem solving a continuous process?
- What is meant by the statement, "Often, it is only possible to find probable causes."?

The Problem-Solving Process

To prepare for discussion, have each person read this section. Lead the group through the seven steps to solving problems. List and discuss each of the steps.

> *Note:* The following information may be used to give the students more experience with analyzing data. Since this information isn't available in *Job Savvy*, permission to make copies for use with the trainees is given. Following the written information, students may test their learning by doing the exercises listed under "Applying What You've Learned."

Data Analysis

The second step in the problem-solving process is gathering data and analyzing it. There are three simple methods for analyzing data. This study will show how frequency tables, percents, and graphs are used to analyze data.

Frequency Tables

There are two types of frequency tables. One table is used for data collection and the other for data summary.

Data Collection Frequency Table

The frequency table for data collection is created by making three columns. The left column should be labeled, "Item," label the middle column "Tally," and the right column "Number." A description of the observation or answer is written under "Item," in the left column, each time something different occurs or a new answer is given. A mark is made in the "Tally" column beside it. This process continues until all observations or data collection is completed. Count the number of marks in the "Tally" column and record in the "Number" column.

The following example shows how a frequency table might look. The data gathered concerns customer complaints about lawn mowers.

DATA COLLECTION FREQUENCY TABLE		
ITEM	TALLY	NUMBER (%)
Motor quits working	1111	5
Handle breaks	1111 1111 1111	14
Starter won't work	111	3
Oil leaks	1111 1111 1	11
Blade falls off	1111 11	7
Tires fall off	1111	4
Controls won't work	1111 1	6

©1993, JIST Works, Inc. • Indianapolis, Indiana

The frequency table provides information that can be found quickly. Looking at the table, one can easily see the problem that occurs most frequently is that the "handle breaks." The problem that occurs the least is that the "starter won't work." This table provides the maximum (14) and minimum (3) numbers. The difference between the maximum and the minimum figures is called the range. In this example the range is 11.

Percentages

Percent can be defined as a fraction with a denominator of 100. The percent (%) sign is substituted for the decimal in the fraction. Thus, 83% could be expressed as 83/100. Percents help compare items.

Since percents have the common denominator of 100, they can be added, subtracted, multiplied, and divided. For example, if 25% of a store's customers buy something on Friday and 28% buy on Saturday, you can say that 53% of all sales are made on Friday and Saturday. In this example, it is possible to add 25% and 28% because they have a common denominator.

Percents for frequency tables are calculated by dividing the number of observations of one item by the total number of observations and multiplying by 100. (The data gathered about a problem is 100 percent (100%) of all observations of one item by the total number of observations or answers.) Below is the formula to figure percentage.

$$\frac{\text{One Item}}{\text{Total}} \times 100 = \text{Percentage}(\%)$$

Here is an example of how to calculate percents. The frequency table in the previous exercise showed 14 customers reported broken handles. The total in the "Number" column is 50 customer complaints. Place these numbers in the formula like so:

$$\frac{14}{50} = .28 \times 100 = 28\%$$

Using this example, you could say that 28% of all customer complaints are due to broken handles. Percents provide information necessary to complete a data summary frequency table such as the following figure.

DATA SUMMARY FREQUENCY TABLE		
ITEM	NUMBER	PERCENT (%)
Motor quits working	5	10
Handle breaks	14	28
Starter won't work	3	6
Oil leaks	11	22
Blade falls off	7	14
Tires fall off	4	8
Controls won't work	6	12

By using percents it is possible to find the most frequent reasons for customer complaints and add them together. Using the summary table, it is possible to say that 50% of all customer complaints are because the handle breaks (28%) and the oil leaks (22%).

Pareto's 20/80 Rule

An interesting discovery was made by a man named Vilfredo Pareto. He found that there is a disproportionate distribution that seems to exist in many areas of business and economics. This disproportionate distribution is often called Pareto's 20/80 rule. (A specific application is referred to as the ABC Inventory Analysis.[1]) For examples of this rule, 20% of an organization's inventory accounts for 80% of the sales; 20% of customers account for 80% of all sales; 20% of all manufacturing mistakes account for 80% of product defects. In solving problems, it is often true that 20% of people, things, or processes cause about 70% to 80% of a problem.

Graphs

Another way to organize data is by using graphs. Graphs help the eye visualize the data and draw conclusions. It is sometimes easier to interpret data by looking at a graph rather than looking at the numbers in a frequency table. There are several types of graphs. The exercise below illustrates the bar graph.

Bar graphs are one of the most commonly used graphs. They compare quantities. Bar graphs work well to display data in frequency tables. The bars allow comparison between items listed in a frequency table. The following bar chart displays the data in the customer complaint frequency table. The bar chart illustrates which complaints are made most frequently. By looking at the chart, it is easy to see which bars are the highest and by comparison which complaints occur most often.

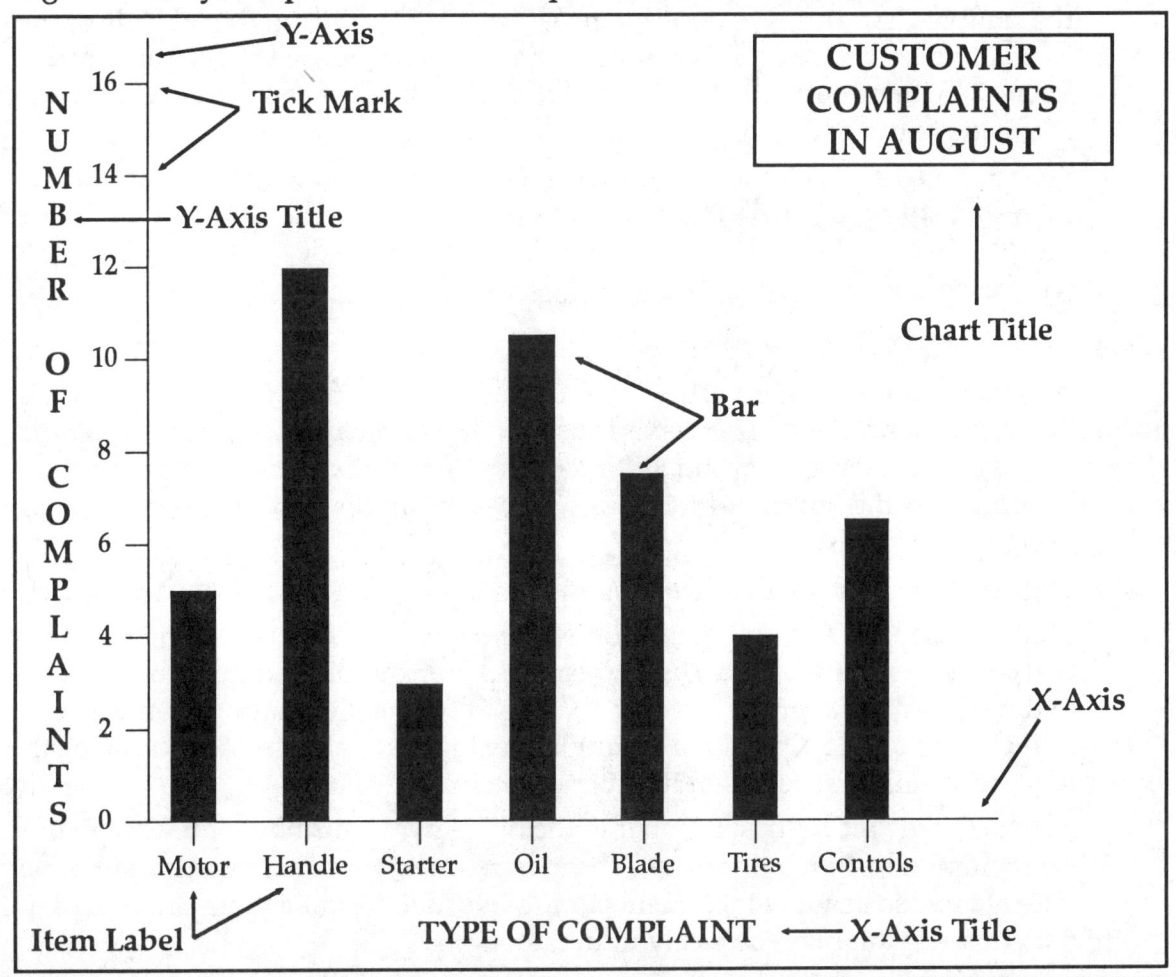

To know how to create a chart, one must understand its different parts. (Notice that the different parts of the bar chart are labeled.) Look at this chart for reference when following the steps explaining how to draw a bar chart.

Create the X-Axis Scale

The X-axis is the horizontal line on the chart. In business charts, the X-axis is normally a person, place, event, or time period. In other words, the X-axis isn't used to display numbers.

- **Step 1:** Count the number of items to be displayed on the X-axis. In the sample chart, there were seven items.
- **Step 2:** Draw the X-axis line by drawing a horizontal line 6 inches long about 1-1/2 inches from the bottom of the paper. A standard size piece of paper is 8-1/2 inches × 11 inches. Using 6 inches allows a 1-1/4 inch border on each side of the chart.
- **Step 3:** To calculate the distance between each tick mark on the X-axis line, divide 6 inches plus 2 by the number of items to be plotted on the X-axis. Adding two to the number of items provides space between the first tick mark and the Y-axis. An equal amount of space is reserved on the right side of the X-axis line. This is calculated for the sample chart by: 2 + 7 = 9 6"/9 = 6/9" = 2/3".
- **Step 4:** Draw the tick marks plotted for each item on the X-axis line. Use the distance calculated in Step 3 to measure the space between each tick mark. For the sample chart this was done by measuring 2/3 inch from the left side of the X-axis line and making a tick mark. This is where the first item was plotted. Every 2/3 inch another tick mark was drawn until all seven tick marks for the X-axis were drawn.
- **Step 5:** Label the tick marks on the X-axis using a one-word description for each item to be plotted. Write the description under the tick marks. In the sample chart the labels Motor, Handle, Starter, Oil, Blade, Tires, and Controls were used.

Create the Y-Axis Scale

The Y-axis represents the vertical line on the chart. In business charts, this is normally a range of numbers. The Y-axis is used to find the value for each item on the X-axis. This value is marked or plotted directly above the tick marks on the X-axis.

The number at the bottom of the Y-axis will typically be zero. Follow the steps below to create the Y-axis.

- **Step 1:** Draw an 8 inch vertical line starting at the left point of the X-axis line.
- **Step 2:** Calculate the range of numbers to be used to determine the scale for the Y-axis tick marks. Take the highest value for the plotted items and round to the highest number divisible by 10, 100, 1,000, etc. depending on the values of the items on the X-axis. For example, the highest value in the sample chart is 14, so the highest rounded number of the range is 20.
- **Step 3:** Divide the highest number in the range by the number you want to use for increments of each tick mark. The sample chart uses increments of two. Be creative to decide what increments to use in order to make your chart display data in a way that will be easily understood.

- **Step 4:** Divide the highest number in your range by that increment. Divide 8 inches for the axis by this number. Measure this distance from the intersection of the X- and Y-axis and draw a tick mark. Measure the same distance for all tick marks on the Y-axis. Twenty is the highest number in the sample chart range and 2 is the increment. Dividing 20 by the increment results in the value of 10. You then divide 8 inches by 10. This gives you 8/10 inch or 4/5 inch. Measure this distance for the tick marks on the Y-axis.

- **Step 5:** Next label the tick marks. Start by labeling the intersection of the X- and Y-axis zero. Then label the values of the increments and put these numbers beside the tick marks above the intersection on the Y-axis. Add the incremental values to the tick mark values to calculate the number to place at each tick mark. The Y-axis on the sample chart begins at zero with increments of two. Therefore the first tick mark value is 2. Add the increment value (two) to the tick mark value two. Put four beside the next tick mark. Continue adding the increment value to each tick mark value. Do this until 20.

Plot Values for the X-Axis Items

Use the Y-axis scale to plot values for the X-axis items. Look for the increments on the Y-axis scale that equal the item values on the X scale. If there is not a number equal to that value, place the number on the axis range where it would be approximately equal to that value. Working in a horizontal direction, place tick marks above the the items on the X-axis. Repeat this process for all the X-axis items.

In the sample chart, the value for Motor is five. Since there is no tick mark with the value five on the Y-axis, assume it is between four and six. Place a dot or some other mark at this point directly above Motor on the X-axis.

Draw the bars

Draw a bar about half the size of the increments between the X-axis tick marks. The top of the bar is the point plotted and marked for the item as described in Step 3. Draw the bar so that the X tick mark is in the middle.

Label the Chart Titles

There are three titles in a chart. The first title explains what the chart is about. The second title labels the X-axis describing the items plotted on the axis. The third title describes what values are plotted on the Y-axis.

In the sample chart, the title is "Customer Complaints in August." The X-axis title is "Type of Complaint," and the Y-axis title is "Number of Complaints."

Applying What You've Learned

This exercise allows practice using frequency tables, percents, and graphs.

Diane works for a business of 2,300 employees that manufactures pretzels. Her quality circle team is trying to solve the problem of how to reduce accidents at the plant. Diane was asked to compile data about the type of injuries that have occurred at the plant during the past month. The company nurse provided the following monthly accident report.

ACCIDENT REPORT—TASTEE PRETZELS, INC.—OCTOBER

DATE	PERSON	DESCRIPTION OF ACCIDENT
1	Smith	Tripped over ladder-sprained ankle
3	Rogers	Hand caught in machine-large cut
3	Jackson	Slipped on mopped floor-injured back
5	Cortez	Fell down steps-injured back
6	Gerber	Brushed against ovens-burned hand
8	Mitchell	Tripped over boxes-sprained ankle
9	Walls	Didn't use gloves-burned hand
10	Washington	Fell from ladder-broke leg
12	Ott	Lifted heavy box-injured back
13	Wallace	Solvent splashed-eye injured
13	Michaels	Fell on steps-injured back
15	Chavez	Running and tripped-injured back
16	Jones	Tripped over ladder-sprained ankle
18	DiFabbio	Hand caught in machine-large cut
19	Buzan	Slipped on mopped floor-injured back
20	Leveau	Fell down steps-injured back
21	Tillet	Brushed against ovens-burned hand
22	Corte	Tripped over boxes-sprained ankle
23	Davidson	Didn't wear gloves-burned hand
26	Cardamone	Fell from ladder-broke leg
27	Holt	Lifted heavy box-injured back
30	Lilly	Solvent splashed-eye injured
30	Harris	Fell on steps-injured back
31	DeBono	Running and tripped-injured back

©1993, JIST Works, Inc. • Indianapolis, Indiana

- Create a frequency table for Diane that summarizes the data in the report. Draw the table in this space.

- Calculate percents for each item listed in the frequency table. Add another column to the frequency table in Step 1. Write each of the percents in that column.

- Draw a bar chart using the frequency table in this exercise. Use this space to draw the graph.

Creative Thinking

> *Note:* Many people believe that they have no creative ability. Often creativity is associated with gifted musicians, artists, or authors. Encourage your students to view creativity in a broader sense. Help them see the creative potential in each person. Finding a solution to any problem is creative.

Have the group read "Creative Thinking." Encourage them to do the exercises in *Job Savvy*. The solutions to the exercises are at the end of the chapter.

Additional Activity: Toothpick Creations

Divide into groups of three. Give each group a box of flat toothpicks. Have them create as many different shapes as possible using the toothpicks.

Additional Activity: Guest Speaker

Ask an inventor or entreprenaur to speak to the class concerning how they discovered and developed their idea.

Additional Activity: Creative Problem Solving

Using the following problem, brainstorm all types of ways to solve the problem. Encourage outlandish solutions. Then attempt to make each solution workable.

> *Problem:* Since the new pizza place at the end of the block opened, the Burger Castle, where you work has had less business. The manager has asked all employees for ideas to increase business.

Summary

Read the summary at the end of the chapter and use the following questions for class discussion.

- Why is problem solving so important to employers?
- What is meant by creative thinking?
- Why is it important to use all seven steps in the problem- solving process?

Chapter Nine Endnote

1 James Evans et al., *Applied Production and Operations Management*, (West Publishing Co., St. Paul, Minn., 1987).

Chapter Ten

Ethics: Doing the Right Thing

Chapter Purpose

> *It is vital to understand that making ethical decisions isn't always easy. Sometimes the ethical answer isn't obvious. The "right" decision can bring conflict with another person. This chapter gives guidelines for making choices when the answers may not be clear. The chapter presents case studies involving ethical problems. Through class discussion your students will prepare for real problems that they will most certainly face in the work world.*

A secretary uses the company telephone to call friends long distance. A mechanic slips a wrench into a lunchbox and takes it home. A marketing representative carries a company secret to a competitor. A salesperson adds a few extra miles to the monthly travel report. Each of these situations deals with ethics.

©1993, JIST Works, Inc. • Indianapolis, Indiana

Ethics are rules we use to make decisions about life. Society sets certain standard ethical rules. As members of society, all people are expected to observe these rules. To ignore these rules in the workplace could result in disciplinary action or even dismissal. In some cases, criminal punishment could result.

> *Note:* I included this chapter because it is important for new workers to understand how to make a sound ethical choice. Keep in mind that every person won't choose the same answer to an ethical problem. Each individual's background influences their beliefs about what is right and wrong. It is important for discussion purposes that you encourage free exchange of ideas. Invite differing views as the group seeks to solve these ethical dilemmas.

The chapter ends with a discussion of several ethical problems common in the workplace. Each person needs to be aware of their responsibility to conduct themselves properly in their job situation. Non-ethical behavior can result in dismissal but ethical behavior will bring about the respect of co-workers and superiors. Most of all, it will increase self-respect.

What Are Ethics?

Read the introduction and discuss the meaning of ethics. Use the following questions to guide this discussion.

- How are ethical principles formed?
- Why are ethical principles important in a job situation?
- How could ethical choices affect one's job situation?
- What complicates making ethical choices in work situations?
- Who could your ethical decision affect in a work situation?

Additional Activity: Ethics Quiz

To illustrate the difficulty people may experience in viewing ethical and non-ethical behavior, ask the group to complete the following exercise. True or false are the only answers allowed.

TRUE	FALSE	ETHIC STATEMENT
		Breaking the law is always wrong.
		Speeding is sometimes necessary.
		All drug sales should be illegal.
		The use of alcohol is legal.
		Every citizen should give to charity.
		Accepting charity is a humbling experience.
		Killing is always wrong.
		Wars are sometimes necessary.

Exercise: **Journal Assignment**

As a journal article have students record some ethical values they have and what influenced them in forming these values.

What Is Ethical Behavior?

Allow time for each individual to fill out the list under this section. Ask individuals to share their lists regarding each of the three areas. As they share their reasons, use a flip chart or overhead to compile the lists for the entire group to view.

Ethical Decision-Making Problems

Allow time for each individual to read each case study in this section. Discuss the three basic problems that can cause obstacles in making the proper decision in the workplace. Consider the following questions under each area.

Not knowing what is expected
- Why might you not know how to react in a particular situation?
- How could you handle an unfamiliar situation?

Conflicts in ethical standards
- Who might you conflict with in the workplace?
- How can you behave ethically without causing more conflict?

Dilemmas about a situation
- Why are some decisions more difficult to make than others?
- How would you make a decision in an unclear situation?

©1993, JIST Works, Inc. • Indianapolis, Indiana

After reading the case studies, students should write a brief description of how they would handle each situation.

> *Note:* Don't discuss the situations at this time. This information will be used later in the chapter.

Guidelines for Making Ethical Decisions

Using this section, discuss each of the questions one may ask to make an ethical decision. Emphasize that before reaching a decision a person should consider more than one of the questions. Listed below are some important issues to stress.

Is it legal?
- Each employee is responsible for their own behavior. A court of law will not excuse an illegal act resulting from a work order.

How will it make you feel about yourself?
- Keeping one's self-respect is vital in maintaining one's self-esteem. The importance of self-esteem in the job market was addressed in chapter 6.

How do others feel about it?
- Seek advice from people you respect. Talking to people with varying viewpoints provides a wider scope of choices.
- Be willing to listen to someone who disagrees with you.
- Accept responsibility for your decision. Realize that only you (not your supervisors, instructors, counselors, etc.) will be held accountable for the action taken.

How would you feel if the whole world knew about it?
- If the respect others have for you will decrease from your behavior, don't do it.
- Don't assume that no one will find out. Even if they don't, you will still be afraid they will.

Does the behavior make sense?
- Calmly consider the effects of this behavior.
- Will it harm others? This could include physical, mental, or financial well-being.
- Will it harm you? What if you get caught? Is it really worth the risk of punishment?

Is the situation fair to everyone involved?
- Probably not everyone will benefit from your actions in an equal way, but trying to maintain balance is important.
- Making a decision that greatly benefits one individual (especially yourself) at the expense of another, is very unwise.

Will the people in authority at your organization approve?
- Getting information about the situation from authorities (supervisors, managers, employers, the company's lawyer) will allow you to see the organization's viewpoint.
- Authorities are not always ethical. As an individual, you are still responsible for your actions.

How would you feel if someone did the same thing to you?
- Think of yourself as the "other" person. How do you want to be treated?

Will something bad happen if you don't make a decision?
- Perhaps the best approach is to do nothing. You may remain uninvolved at times but should consider some questions with this course of action: Do you have all the facts? Is someone else in authority handling the situation? Will the situation resolve itself with time?

> *Note: Doing nothing when you know someone is being harmed will only cause more problems.*

Applying What You've Learned

Divide into small groups. Have each group discuss the three case studies. Using the guidelines for making ethical decisions discussed earlier, have each group write an explanation of each case study. Each group should give reasons for their solutions. In the large group setting, share the answers and thoughts for the explanations given.

Allow time for each individual to reevaluate their behavioral choices of the five situations presented at the beginning of this chapter (pages 142-144). The ethical questions should be applied in each situation. Trainees should record any changes they might make as well as the reasons for their choices. Now as a group, go over each of these situations. What were the solutions in each case? What ethical questions influenced decisions? Was anyone influenced to change their original choices?

Common Ethical Problems

List and discuss the seven ethical problems. Consider the important points under each topic. As each problem is discussed, add additional ways employees can cheat the company.

Favoring friends or relatives
- As an employee benefit, a company may provide special discounts to employees' families. It is important for employees to know what these benefits are and to whom they apply.

Cheating the employer out of time
- In any business, time is money. Using work time for other purposes robs the company.

©1993, JIST Works, Inc. • Indianapolis, Indiana

Stealing from the company
- Taking "little" items multiplies when many employees are involved.

Abusing drugs and alcohol
- Many companies require drug testing as a part of their employment qualifications.

Violating matters of confidentiality
- It is important that employees know the company's policy on confidentiality.

Knowing about other employees' unethical behaviors
- Consider all the consequences if you decide to report another worker's unethical work behavior.
- Gossip should never be the basis for reporting misconduct.

Violating the organization's policies
- Knowing the company's policies is important. Breaking these policies could result in disciplinary action.

> *Note: If you are training for a particular organization, explain that company's policy in each of these areas. What type of disciplinary action would the company take?*

Applying What You've Learned

Divide into small groups. Work together solving the three case studies. As a large group, discuss each situation and the reasons for each solution.

Summary

In completing this chapter, read together the summary and use the following questions for discussion.
- Why are an employee's ethics important to a company?
- What can result in an employee's unethical behavior?
- Why is it sometimes difficult to make ethical decisions?

Chapter Eleven

Getting Ahead on the Job

CHAPTER PURPOSE

> *Getting a job is work. Keeping that job is even more work. But most workers want even more. They want to advance on their jobs. Often, however, they are confused about what they need to do to get ahead on the job. This chapter explains what employees need to do to gain job advances.*

My friend Shannon has worked at a day care center for two years. As a teacher's aide working with young children, Shannon believes there is no possibility for any type of promotion. The pay rate is low, and no benefits are offered. Discouraged by this job situation, Shannon is ready for a change.

©1993, JIST Works, Inc. • Indianapolis, Indiana

Workers expect to be rewarded for their job performance. In the work world rewards are usually pay increases and job promotions. Often the new worker has unrealistic ideas of when and why these rewards should come. This chapter presents information on pay raises and promotions. Its approach is very general since different companies' policies vary so much.

> *Note:* If you are training for a particular organization, this would be an excellent time to present their policies in these areas.

Young workers may find the ideas for career development helpful. Learning to set realistic career goals early can help new worker progress. By spending some time thinking about these goals, they may approach their career in a much more organized way.

Few people remain in the same job their entire work experience. Knowing how and why to leave a job is important not only to trainees, but experienced workers as well. The final section discusses reasons for leaving a job and how to tell the company that you are quitting.

What Concerns a New Worker

Have trainees read the chapter introduction. Ask the questions "How many of you want to take home the pay you get now for the rest of your life? How many of you want to stay in the same position in your company for the rest of your life?" Pay raises and promotions are important to all workers.

Additional Activity: Employer Feedback

As an introduction to this chapter, brainstorm a list of ways an employer lets a worker know that they are doing a good job. (Pay raises and promotions will probably be among the suggestions.)

Getting A Raise

Discuss the six common instances when employers give pay raises. Be sure the trainees understand that not every company follows these same policies. They should ask their supervisor questions about their company's pay raise policy.

Additional Activity: To Raise or Not to Raise

Use the questions under each heading to guide group discussion. You may make up a separate worksheet for this activity. Give an "open book" test. After the individuals have answered the questions, go through the worksheet sharing the information learned.

Completion of Probation
- Why might a raise be given after a worker completes probation? How long can the probation period last?

Incentive Increases
- How does this method determine a worker's raise?
- How often might a worker be evaluated using this method?
- Why might the ability to get along with others be important in receiving an incentive increase?

Cost of Living Increases
- What is the meaning of inflation?
- What does a cost of living increase do for a worker?

Keep Employees
- Why might an employer offer a raise in an attempt to keep an employee?
- What is the risk to an employee when they approach their employer with the fact that they can get more money in a different job?

Reward for Special Efforts
- What are some added job responsibilities that could result in a pay raise?
- What are some new skills an employee might acquire that could result in a pay raise?

New Assignments
- Why does a pay raise often accompany a promotion?
- Discuss the information in the box, "The Difference Between Wage and Salary." Emphasize that salaried workers often have more responsibilities.
- Be sure the group understands that a salaried worker does not receive any overtime pay although they may be required to work more than an 8-hour day. Many entry-level employees do not realize this.

Applying What You've Learned

Divide into groups of three to four members. Assign the four case studies for each group to discuss. Use the questions as guide lines for their discussions. Have each group share their opinions about each case study.

Additional Activity: Role Play

In addition to answering the questions concerning each case study, assign one of the case studies to each group. (You may need to assign more than one group to a case study.) Each group should write out a role play between the person and supervisor in the case study. In each case, the person should ask for a pay raise and give the reasons for the raise. Members of each group could present their role play to the entire class.

Getting Promoted

Allow time for each individual to read this section. What are the two major criteria for promotions? (Be sure the group understands the meaning of each term.) Use the following questions as a guide to discuss the reasons for wanting to be promoted.

©1993, JIST Works, Inc. • Indianapolis, Indiana

Increased Pay
- If a pay raise is given with a promotion, what might a worker assume about the new position?
- Why might a worker in a salaried promotion position not get as large a raise as expected?

More Respect
- Why does a promotion increase a person's status?

Better Assignments
- How does a promotion result in a greater challenge to a worker?

Improved Self-Esteem
- Why does a promotion increase one's self-esteem?

Additional Activity: Promotability
Brainstorm a list of items that could influence a supervisor to promote an employee.

Use the following questions to discuss how to get promoted.

- Who knows about job openings within your organizaon?
- What is meant by the term "posting?"
- What is meant by the term "networking?"
- Who might be included in your network?
- What can a worker do to develop a good reputation?
- How can a worker "create their own job?"

Exercise: Journal Assignment
As a journal article, have the group complete the following statement and give reasons for the statement. "I should be promoted to the position of _____ because I _____."

When Promotions Occur

Allow time for individuals to read and do this section. Have the group make a list of all the skills a worker needs to get a promotion. Post this list. Use the list to do "Applying What You've Learned."

Applying What You've Learned

Divide into small groups. Have the groups do the case studies using the posted list of skills to make their decisions. Then have the groups share their choices and the reasons in each case. There may be some disagreement among the groups, but there need not be a consensus. Use this opportunity to illustrate that making a decision about promoting someone in the organization is not always easy.

Career Development

Discuss the meaning of the term "career development." Together go through the topics listed under career development.

Additional Activity: CEI

Using the CEI, a career interest test, have individuals explore career choices. The CEI, Career Exploration Inventory, is designed for exploration of work, leisure activities, and education or learning. This simple, self-scoring device can help identify career areas of interest. It is available from JIST Works, Inc.

Additional Activity: Progress Report

Divide into groups of three. Each group should choose an entry-level job. Using the questions under the bulleted section "Develop a Career Path," have each group write a career progression plan.

Exercise: Journal Assignment

Ask each student to record a career plan for themselves.

Additional Activity: Video Presentation

Show the video titled *Job Survival Skills*. This 18-minute video has two parts, "How to Avoid Getting Fired" and "How to Get Ahead." It is available through JIST Works, Inc.

Leaving a Job

Discuss the reasons for leaving a job. Discuss the suggestions for preparing to leave a job.

Additional Activity: Make Like a Tree and Leaf

Divide into small study groups. Have each group answer the following questions about leaving a job.

- Name some reasons for leaving a job.
- How soon should you tell your employer that you are leaving? If you aren't sure how to resign, who could advise you?
- What are the reasons for having another job waiting before resigning from your present job?
- Imagine that you are leaving your job because your supervisor is treating you unfairly. How do you tell your supervisor that you are quitting?
- What are some things you may be required to do before you leave the job?
- Why is it important to leave a job with good relationships if at all possible?

Applying What You've Learned

Divide into groups of three. Read and discuss the two case studies and come to a group decision about each case. Ask each group to share their answers.

©1993, JIST Works, Inc. • Indianapolis, Indiana

Summary

Read the summary of the chapter and use the following questions for class discussion.

- What are some things a worker can do to obtain promotions and pay raises?
- What is the difference between wage and salary?
- How can planning help in your career development?
- What are some important things to remember about leaving a job?

Other Titles Available

JIST publishes a variety of books on careers and job search topics. Please consider ordering one or more from your dealer, local bookstore, or directly from JIST.

Orders from Individuals: Please use the form below (or provide the same information) to order additional copies of this or other books listed on this page. You are also welcome to send us your order (please enclose money order, check, or credit card information), or simply call our toll free number at **1-800-648-JIST** or **1-317-264-3720**. Our FAX number is **1-317-264-3709** or *toll free* **1-800-JIST-FAX**. Qualified schools and organizations may request our catalog and obtain information on quantity discounts (we have over 400 career-related books, videos, and other items). Our offices are open weekdays 8 a.m. to 5 p.m. local time and our address is:

JIST Works, Inc. • 720 North Park Avenue • Indianapolis, IN 46202-3431

QTY	BOOK TITLE	TOTAL ($)
_____	*Getting the Job You Really Want*, J. Michael Farr • ISBN 0-942784-15-4 • $9.95	_____
_____	*The Very Quick Job Search: Get a Good Job in Less Time*, J. Michael Farr • ISBN 0-942784-72-3 • $9.95	_____
_____	*America's 50 Fastest Growing Jobs: An Authoritative Information Source* • ISBN 0-942784-61-8 • $10.95	_____
_____	*America's Top 300 Jobs: A Complete Career Handbook* (trade version of the *Occupational Outlook Handbook*) • ISBN 0-942784-45-6 • $17.95	_____
_____	*America's Federal Jobs: A Complete Directory of Federal Career Opportunities* • ISBN 0-942784-81-2 • $14.95	_____
_____	*America's Top Medical Jobs: Good Jobs in Health Related Occupations* • ISBN 1-56370-046-8 • $9.95	_____
_____	*America's Top Technical and Trade Jobs: Good Jobs that Don't Require Four Years of College* • ISBN 1-56370-041-7 • $9.95	_____
_____	*America's Top Office, Management and Sales Jobs: Good Jobs that Offer Advancement and Excellent Pay* • ISBN 1-56370-041-7 • $9.95	_____
_____	*The Resume Solution: How to Write and Use a Resume That Gets Results*, David Swanson • ISBN 0-942784-44-8 • $8.95	_____
_____	*The Job Doctor: Good Advice on Getting a Good Job*, Phillip Norris, Ed.D. • ISBN 0-942784-43-X • $5.95	_____
_____	*The Right Job for You: An Interactive Career Planning Guide*, J. Michael Farr • ISBN 0-942784-73-1 • $9.95	_____
_____	*Exploring Careers: A Young Person's Guide to over 300 Jobs* • ISBN 0-942784-27-8 • $19.95	_____
_____	*Work in the New Economy: Careers and Job Seeking into the 21st Century*, Robert Wegmann • ISBN 0-942784-19-78 • $14.95	_____
_____	*The Occupational Outlook Handbook* • ISBN 0-942784-38-3 • $16.95	_____
_____	*The Enhanced Guide for Occupational Exploration: Descriptions for the 2,500 Most Important Jobs* • ISBN 0-942784-76-6 • $29.95	_____
_____	*U.S. Industrial Outlook '92: Business Forecasts for 350 Industries* • ISBN 1-56370-062-X • $29.95	_____
_____	*The Career Connection: Guide to College Majors and Their Related Careers*, Dr. Fred Rowe • ISBN 0-942784-82-0 • $15.95	_____
_____	*The Career Connection II: Guide to Technical Majors and Their Related Careers*, Dr. Fred Rowe • ISBN 0-942784-83-9 • $13.95	_____
_____	*Dictionary of Occupational Titles*: 2-volume set • ISBN 1-56370-000-X • $39.00	_____
_____	*Standard Industrial Classification Manual* • ISBN 1-56370-064-6 • $35.00	_____
_____	*The Revised Handbook for Analyzing Jobs* • ISBN 1-56370-051-4 • $14.95	_____
_____	*Americans With Disabilities Act: Legal Guide* • ISBN 1-56370-076-X • $17.95	_____
_____	*Americans With Disabilities Act: Resource Directory* • ISBN 1-56370-077-8 • $17.95	_____
_____	*Americans With Disabilities Act: Handbook* • ISBN 1-56370-080-8 • 39.95	_____

Subtotal _____
Sales Tax _____
Shipping: ($3 for first book, $1 for each additional book.) _____
(U.S. Currency only) **TOTAL ENCLOSED WITH ORDER** _____
(Prices subject to change without notice)

___ Check   ___ Money order   Credit Card: ___ MasterCard   ___ VISA   ___ AMEX

Card # (if applies)_____ Exp. Date_____
Name (please print)_____
Name of Organization (if applies) _____
Address _____
City/State/Zip_____
Daytime Telephone (_____)_____—_____

Thank-you for your order!